Holistic Philosophy 102

Physician, Heal Thy Self!

by
Mishaal Mahfuz
Talib El Bey

© 2022
CalifaMedia.com™

Holistic Philosophy 102

© 2022

Califa Media Publishing™

Lafayette, Indiana

Written by

Mishaal Talib Mahfuz El Bey

ISBN-13: 978-1-952828-18-8

ISBN-10: 1-952828-18-X

Available as an electronic book ISBN: 978-1-952828-20-1

All Rights Reserved. Without Prejudice. No Part Of This Book May Be Reproduced Or Transmitted In Any Form By Any Means, Electronic, Photocopying, Mechanical, Recording, Information Storage Or Retrieval System Unless For The Liberation Of Minds And Gaining Knowledge Of Self.

Califa Media
A Moorish Guide Publishing Company
califamedia.com
All Rights, Remedies & Liberties Reserved

Cover Design by Sis. T. Najee-Ullah El
Califa Media Publishing

Main Cover Image: "Maat"
Artist Unknown

Table of Contents

Intro:—1

Chapter 1:—2
Yin and Yang

Chapter 2:—6
Foods for the Seasons

Chapter 3:—8
Minerals

Chapter 4: Squaring the Circle—46
Chief Principles of the Zoroastrian Religion

Chapter 5: Energy Cleansing—49
Balancing the Chakra

Chapter 6: As Above so Below—57
*3 Types of Man (Mind): A Cosmological Guide

Chapter 7: Law and Order—104
*Rules and Regulations

Chapter 8: Reconstruction of unity—107
*Yoga Paths

Chapter 9: Awakening —114
*Gaining

Chapter 10: Rulership—119
*7 Laws of Teaching

Outro:—130

Works cited:—131

Support Your Own!!!—132

Other Titles

by

Mishaal Talib Mahfuz El Bey

Holistic Philosophy 101

Isonimi:The Great Masonic Secret: Master Keys

The Torch: A Guide to S.E.L.F.

Intro:

Holism-the theory that reality is made up of organic or unified wholes that are greater than the simple sum of their parts. Holy-Middle English holy, holi, hali, Old English halig. See kailo; Kailo-whole, uninjured, of good omen, wholesome, health, to consecrate, bless. As is stated by definition and what can be intuitively deduced from one's life experience to be holy is to be whole and to be whole is to tend to all aspects of "self": mentally, physically, emotionally and spiritually. Man is mind; therefore, we have the awesome innate ability to heal, transform and regenerate. A roach will always be such, a dog may learn new tricks, but it'll still bark and lick its own but. The point being that we as human beings are in an extremely privileged position being that through the gift of our divine we will become a better version of what we once were which is the point. Once this is realized and accepted we begin to see and be ourselves as we are all truly meant to be.

Chapter 1:
Yin and Yang

Genesis 5:2, ESV: "Male and female he created them, and he blessed them and named them Man when they were created."

Male Principle

- science
- square
- pyramid
- electricity
- Serotonin increase
- Speeds up action
- Contracts energy
- Sympathetic nervous system
- Acidic bodily condition
- Uses energy
- adrenergic
- thoracolumbar
- Blood flow to brain: decrease
- Contracts vessels
- Blood flow to muscle: increase
- Nervous system action: increase
- Excretory system: decrease
- Digestive system: decrease
- Respiratory system: increase
- Circulatory system: increase
- Reproductive system: decrease
- Spiritual system: decrease
- Kingdom of Gods: decrease
- Pingala nerve
- back
- anus
- Flaccid penis
- Active vaginal muscles
- Solid crystals
- pineal

Female Principle

- art
- circle
- Pyramid
- magnetism
- Melatonin increase
- Slows down action
- Expands energy
- Parasympathetic nervous system
- Alkaline bodily condition
- Gathers energy
- cholinergic
- craniosacral
- Blood flow to brain: increase
- Expands vessels
- Blood flow to muscle: decrease
- Nervous system action: decrease
- Excretory system: increase
- Digestive system: increase
- Respiratory system: decrease
- Circulatory system: decrease
- Reproductive system: increase
- Spiritual system: increase
- Kingdom of Gods: increase
- Ida nerve
- front
- mouth
- Erect penis
- Passive vaginal muscles
- Gas & liquid crystals
- panceas

- kidney
- thyroid
- lungs
- Large intestine
- thymus
- Upper jaw
- Negative energy enters left foot and exits right hand
- Cosmic energy enters right foot and exits left hand
- Positive anger, fear
- Sun, Mars, Mercury
- Fire, air
- electrical
- vertical
- initiative
- visible
- temporal
- exoteric
- East, west
- electromagnetic
- negative
- Osiris (North Pole)
- Nephthys (East Pole)
- Cayenne, mandrake
- Licorice, comfrey
- phoenix
- ape
- gold
- pungent
- Salty taste in foods
- orange
- red
- blue
- frankincense
- lavender
- Oak, cedar

- heart
- spleen
- liver
- Small intestine
- pituitary
- Lower jaw
- Positive energy enters right foot and exits left hand
- Cosmic energy enters left foot and exits right hand
- Love bonding
- Venus, Moon (Sun's reflection)
- Water, earth
- magnetic
- horizontal
- receptive
- visible
- eternal
- esoteric
- North, south
- electromagnetic
- Positive
- Ra (South Pole)
- Isis (West Pole)
- Garlic, ginger
- Mints, blue water lily
- hippopotamus
- crocodile
- silver
- sour
- Sweet taste in foods
- green
- violet
- indigo
- Jasmine, calamus
- pine
- Rose, sandalwood

- Beans, roots, vegetables
- fecundity
- fall
- contractive
- clairvoyance
- nitrogen
- oxygen
- phosphorus
- copper
- tin
- lead
- zinc
- bismuth
- sulfur
- heru
- ra
- cup
- scepter
- Vitamin k
- Vitamin c
- Vitamin a
- Epinephrine
- snake
- To know
- To dare
- action
- resistance
- study
- intrepidity
- Gemini
- libra
- Aquarius
- Aries
- Sagittarius
- Leo

- Fruit, sprouts, sweet, celery
- aridity
- rise
- expansive
- audiovoyance
- carbon
- hydrogen
- sodium
- iron
- nickel
- titanium
- cobalt
- potassium
- magnesium
- hathor
- nu
- Magic wand (caduceus)
- pentacle
- Vitamin e
- Vitamin b
- Vitamin d
- acetylcholine
- vulture
- To will
- To keep silent
- completion
- result
- will
- discretion
- cancer
- Scorpio
- Pisces
- Taurus
- Virgo
- Capricorn

Chapter 2:
Foods for the Seasons

Summer

- basil
- capsicum
- carrots
- coriander
- cucumber
- eggplant
- parsley
- lettuce
- potatoes

- rocket
- squash
- sugar
- snap peas
- corn
- tomatoes
- zucchini
- apples
- apricots

- blackberries
- cherries
- mangoes
- nectarines
- passionfruit
- peaches
- pineapple
- plums
- watermelons

Autumn

- avocadoes
- broccoli
- Brussel sprouts
- cabbage
- turnips
- cauliflower

- fennel
- leeks
- onions
- parsnips
- swedes
- sweet potatoes

- lemons
- limes
- oranges
- ruby grapefruits

Winter

- broccoli
- capsicum
- eggplants
- fennel
- Jerusalem artichokes

- wild mushrooms
- potatoes
- pumpkin
- silver beets
- spinach
- tomatoes

- bananas
- figs
- grapes
- pears
- lemons
- olives

Spring

- artichokes
- asparagus
- avocadoes
- beet root
- broad beans
- garlic
- peas
- potatoes
- sage
- rosemary
- thyme
- tarragon
- strawberries
- kumquats
- kiwi
- raspberries
- rhubarb

Chapter 3:
Minerals

Iron:
Vital for making blood

Deficiency

- Mental problems
- Nervous disorders
- Anemia
- Fatigue
- Poor resistance to disease
- Pale complexion
- Headache

Herbs

- Burdock root
- Catnip
- Cayenne
- Chamomile
- Chickweed
- Devil's claw
- Dong quai
- Eyebright
- Fennel
- Fenugreek
- Horsetail
- Kelp
- Parsley
- Plantain
- Peppermint,
- Sarsaparilla
- Shepherd's purse
- Strawberry leaves
- Uva ursi
- Yellowdock

Foods

- Almonds
- Apricots
- Avocados
- Bananas
- Beans
- Beets
- Lentils
- Millet
- Peaches
- Pears
- Prunes
- Pumpkins
- Raisins
- Rice
- Rye
- Sesame seeds
- Spinach
- Some mineral springs
- Sunflower seeds
- Turnip greens
- Walnuts
- Watercress
- Whole grains

Calcium:

Essential for bones, teeth, muscle action, clotting of blood, and vital activities of the body.

Deficiency

- Soft bones
- Decay
- Nervousness
- Mental problems
- Muscle spasms
- Cramps
- High blood pressure
- Brittle nails
- Eczema
- High cholesterol
- Numbness
- Arthritis
- Heart problems

Herbs

- Aloe root
- Bittersweet root
- Burdock root
- Cayenne,
- Chamomile
- Chickweed
- Chives
- Fennel
- Flaxseed
- Fenugreek
- Hops
- Horsetail,
- Mistletoe
- Peppermint
- Red clover
- Red raspberry leaves
- Rosehip
- Shepherd's purse
- Sorrel
- Toad flax chives
- Yarrow

Foods

- Almonds
- Walnuts
- Raw vegetables
- Beans
- Millet
- Broccoli
- Brussels sprouts
- Oats
- All leafy greens

Phosphorus:

A nutrient for bones and teeth, mentality, nerves, heart and kidney function.

Deficiency

- Skin problems
- Nerve and mental problems
- Anxiety
- Numbness
- Trembling
- Respiratory
- Weakness
- Soft bones
- Poor sexual activity

Herbs

- Alfalfa
- Caraway
- Dulse
- Kelp
- Licorice
- Marigold
- Rosehips
- Rosemary
- Sorrel
- Watercress

Foods

- Asparagus
- Bran
- Corn
- Fruits
- Garlic
- Legumes
- Nuts
- Seeds
- Whole grains

Potassium:

Vital for muscles, heart, digestion, allergies, prevents strokes, stabilizes blood pressure, depression, constipation, diarrhea, mental problems.

Deficiency

- Edema
- Heart problems
- High blood pressure
- Nervous disorders
- Fatigue
- Dry skin
- Chills
- Thirst
- High cholesterol
- Headaches
- Respiratory problems
- Depression
- Constipation
- Diarrhea
- Mental problems

Herbs

- Calamus
- Catnip
- Dandelion
- Dulse
- Eyebright,
- Fennel
- Hops
- Horsetail
- Mullein
- Nettle
- Parsley
- Peppermint
- Plantain
- Red clover
- Rosemary
- Sage
- Skullcap,
- Watercress

Foods

- Apricots
- Avocados
- Bananas
- Brown rice
- Carrots
- Dates
- Figs
- Garlic
- Nuts
- Oranges
- Papayas
- Plantains
- Potatoes
- Raisins
- Squash
- Sunflower seeds,
- Green leafy vegetables
- Whole grains
- Yams

Choline:

Essential for digestion and liver.

Deficiency

- Poor digestion
- Imbalanced body fluid

Herbs

- Alfalfa
- Betony
- Burdock
- Chickweed
- Dandelion
- Kelp
- Myrrh
- Nettle
- Spirulina

Foods

- Asparagus
- Avocadoe
- Cabbage
- Celery
- Cucumber
- Endive
- Kale
- Oats
- Pineapple
- Tomatoes
- Turnips

Sulphur:

A nutrient for skin, nails, hair, disinfects blood, helps resist bacteria.

Deficiency

- Skin problems
- Blemishes
- Rashes, split ends
- Brittle nails

Herbs

- Asafetida
- Broom
- Eyebright
- Horseradish
- Irish moss
- Pimpernel

Foods

- Brussels sprouts
- Cabbage
- Celery
- Kale
- Onions
- Plantain
- Soybeans
- String beans
- Turnips
- Wheat germ

Iodine:

Essential for regulation of mental and physical activity, healthy skin and thyroid, metabolizes, fat.

Deficiency

- Digestion problems
- Asthma
- Female and male sex activity
- Poor bone growth
- Confusion
- Eye problems
- Memory loss
- Tremors
- Tooth grinding
- Hypertension
- Convulsions

Herbs

- Black walnut hulls
- Iceland moss,
- Jojoba
- Kelp
- Sarsaparilla
- Watercress

Foods

- Asparagus
- Garlic
- Lima beans
- Mushrooms
- Sesame seeds
- Soybeans
- Spinach
- Squash
- Turnip greens

Manganese:

Vital for digestion nerves, brain, regulates blood sugar, bone growth, metabolism, reproduction and muscles.

Deficiency

- Digestion problems
- Asthma
- Female and male sex activity
- Poor bone growth
- Confusion
- Eye problems
- Memory loss
- Tremors
- Tooth grinding
- Hypertension
- Convulsions

Herbs

- Alfalfa
- Burdock root
- Broom
- Chickweed
- Dandelion
- Eyebright
- Fennel
- Fenugreek
- Hops
- Horsetail
- Mullein
- Parsley
- Primrose
- Wintergreen
- Yarrow
- Yellow dock

Foods

- Apricots
- Avocados
- Beets
- Blueberries
- Brussels sprouts
- Garlic
- Grapefruit
- Nuts
- Oranges
- Peas
- Pineapples
- Spinach
- All green leafy vegetables

Zinc:

A vital nutrient for cell and tissue growth, prostate, healing wounds and burns, helps taste and smell, vital for enzymes.

Deficiency

- Impaired sexual functions
- Acne
- Hair loss
- High cholesterol
- Recurrent colds
- White spots on toes and/or fingernails
- Poor sense of taste and smell
- Slow healing
- Poor resistance to disease
- Impotence
- Fatigue
- Memory problems

Herbs

- Cayenne
- Chickweed
- Dandelion root
- Eyebright
- Hops
- Milk thistle
- Mullein
- Nettle
- Parsley
- Rose hips
- Sage
- Sarsaparilla
- Skullcap

Foods

- Kelp
- Nuts
- Pumpkin
- Spirulina
- Sunflower seeds
- Wheat germ
- Green leafy vegetables

Chromium:

An essential nutrient. Regulates levels of manganese. Vital for digestion of protein and glucose. Stabilizes blood sugar

Deficiency

- Diabetes
- Low blood sugar
- Heart dis-ease
- Anxiety
- Fatigue
- Hardening of arteries

Herbs

- Alfalfa
- Catnip
- Horsetail
- Kelp
- Licorice
- Nettle
- Oat straw
- Red clover
- Sarsaparilla
- Spirulina
- Yarrow

Foods

- Beans
- Brown rice
- Corn
- Mushrooms
- Potatoes
- Whole grains

Selenium:

Essential for improving liver function, reducing energy loss, protecting body from toxins, aids the prostate, is an antioxidant.

Deficiency

- Liver damage
- Digestive problems
- Muscle weakness
- Cancer
- Fatigue
- Infections
- High cholesterol

Herbs

- Alfalfa
- Burdock root
- Catnip
- Cayenne
- Chamomile
- Chickweed
- Fennel
- Fenugreek
- Ginseng
- Hawthorn berry
- Hops
- Horsetail
- Kelp
- Lemon grass
- Milk thistle
- Nettle
- Parsley
- Sarsaparilla
- Yellow dock

Foods

- Brazil nuts
- Broccoli
- Brown rice
- Garlic
- Mushrooms
- Onions
- Spirulina
- Vegetables
- Whole grains

Lithium:

Vital for nerves and brain.

Deficiency

- Mental problems
- Nervous disorders

Herbs

- Kelp

Foods

- Seawater
- Some natural mineral springs

Vanadium:

Vital for sugar and insulin production, metabolism, bones and teeth.

Deficiency

- Heart and kidney
- Disease
- Diabetes

Herbs

- Dill

Foods

- Olives
- Radishes
- Snap beans
- Whole grains

Magnesium:

Promotes mineral absorption, digestive enzyme activity; helps bone formation; helps metabolize carbohydrates, helps dissolve kidney stones.

Deficiency

- Nervousness
- Irritability
- Rapid heartbeat
- Insomnia
- Tantrums
- Asthmas
- Fatigue
- Pain
- Depression
- Seizures
- Bone loss

Herbs

- Alfalfa
- Dandelion root
- Lemon grass
- Mullein
- Nettle
- Oat straw
- Parsley
- Peppermint
- Red clover
- Sage
- Shepherd's purse
- Yarrow
- Yellow dock

Foods

- Apples
- Apricots
- Bananas
- Brown rice
- Cantaloupe
- Figs
- Garlic
- Grapefruit
- Lemons
- Lima beans
- Millet
- Nuts

- Black-eyed peas
- Sesame seeds
- Soybeans
- Whole grains
- Green leafy vegetables

Common Herbs:

Alfalfa (Medicago sativa) (Herbs and leaves):

Allergies, anemia, appetite (improve), arthritis, bad breath, blood purifier, bursitis, colon, cramps, diabetes, digestive disorders, endurance, energy, flu, fractures, gout, hay fever, hypoglycemia, kidneys, lactation, morning sickness, nausea, pituitary gland, rheumatism, senility, teeth, ulcers, uterus, vitality

Because alfalfa is deep-rooted, it picks up the trace minerals in the soil. It contains eight essential digestive enzymes and eight essential amino acids of protein. It is very rich in vitamins and minerals including vitamin u for peptic ulcers. It is used for a blood thinner, and a kidney cleanser. Athletes use this herb for endurance & energy.

Aloe vera (aloe species) (leaves):

Abrasions, acne, appetite, athlete's foot, burns, cankers, colon, constipation, digestive disorders, ear infection, eczema, fractures, hemorrhoids, liver, mouth sores, poison ivy, psoriasis, tonsillitis, uterus, worms,

Aloe vera is good for chronic constipation-especially in older people. Excellent used as a douche for vaginal discharge and irritation. Especially good for acid burns. It contains allantoin which gives it its healing properties.

Caution: for burns, make sure the preparation does not contain lanolin, as this will intensify the burn. Aloe vera should not be taken during the first 3 months of pregnancy. Aloe vera needs to be stabilized in order to retain its active properties.

Barberry (berberis vulgaris) (root bark):

Anemia, appetite, arthritis, bladder, blood pressure, blood purifier, boils, colon, constipation, diarrhea, digestive disorders, douche, fever, gall bladder, gall stones, gas, gums, heart, heartburn, jaundice, kidneys, liver, mouth sores, rheumatism, skin problems, sore throat, spleen, vagina.

Barberry improves the appetite by promoting bile secretion. It will help eliminate gas when used with one-part wild yam. It has also been used for high blood pressure as it dilates the blood vessels. The tea is used as a mouth wash. A low dose stimulates the heart muscle.

Caution: a high dose slows down the heart muscle and also the respiratory system and could possibly constrict the bronchial tubes.

Bayberry (myrica cerifera) (root bark):

Canker, childhood diseases, circulation, colds, colon, cuts, diarrhea, digestive disorders, eyes, fever, gargle, hay fever, hemorrhage, hoarseness, leucorrhea, lumbago, lungs, menstruation, miscarriage, mucous membranes, sinus congestion, sore throat, thyroid, ulcers, uterus (prolapsed), varicose veins, wounds

Bayberry is an astringent and tonic. Helps stop bleeding from lungs, uterus, and colon. Can be used as a poultice for external sores, and the powder can be used as a snuff for nasal congestion & sinus problems. The tea is used as a gargle for sore throat. It improves circulation.

Caution: large doses could cause nausea or vomiting.

Bee pollen (polen grandular) (pollen)

Allergies, asthma, endurance, energy, hay fever, hypoglycemia, longevity, prostate glands, vitality

Because of its nutritive value, it is a good source of quick energy. For allergies, start with small doses and gradually build up to large doses as the body builds up a resistance to the allergen.

Bistort (polygonum bistorta) (root):

Acne, bed wetting, bleeding, diarrhea, douche, gums, hemorrhage, insect bites, menstruation, skin problems, mouth sores, ulcers, vagina, worms, wounds

Bistort is an astringent. It has been used for mouthwash and gargle, for gum sores, inflammation of the mouth, and sore throat. It helps stop bleeding. It expels worms from the body.

Black cohosh (cimicifuga racemose) (root):

Arthritis, asthma, bee stings, blood pressure, blood purifier, bronchitis, circulation, convulsions, cramps, coughs, diabetes, diarrhea, epilepsy, headaches, heart, hormones (female), hot flashes, insect bites, kidneys, liver, lumbago, lungs, menopause, menstruation, nervous disorders, rheumatism, skin problems, smoking problems, snake bites, thyroid, uterus

Black cohosh is good for almost all female problems. It is a natural supplier of estrogen.

Caution: if headaches occur while taking this herb, the body probably has sufficient estrogen and the herb should be discontinued. Herbs containing progesterone such as sarsaparilla and ginseng may be used.

Black walnut (julgans nigra) (hulls, leaves):

Boils, cold sores, diarrhea, douche, eczema, lactation (bark), leucorrhea, mouth sores, parasites, poison ivy, poison oak, ringworm, skin rashes, teeth, vagina, venereal disease, worms

Black walnut has been used successfully in a tincture or extract for poison ivy, ringworm, and other types of skin problems. It may also be used as a poultice or taken internally. The powder may be used for brushing the teeth to help restore the enamel. When this herb is taken with formula #7, it will kill most parasites in the body.

Blessed thistle (cnicus benedictus) (herb):

Appetite, arthritis, constipation, digestive disorders, female problems, fever, gall bladder, gas, headache, hormones (female), kidneys, lactation, leucorrhea, liver, lungs, menstrual cramps, migraine headaches, urinary disorders

Blessed thistle has been used to increase and enrich the milk in nursing mothers. This herb can be used for female problems when Black cohosh cannot be tolerated. Good for all urinary, pulmonary, and liver disorders. When blessed thistle is given to girls before the onset of puberty, it will help to alleviate future cramping.

Blue cohosh (caulophyllum thalictroides (root):

Bladder infection, blood pressure, blood purifier, childbirth, colic, convulsions, cramps, diabetes, douche, epilepsy, heart, kidneys, leucorrhea, menstruation, nervous disorders, smoking, vagina, water retention.

This herb is formerly known as "Lydia Pinkhams." It stimulates the uterine muscle during childbirth. The pueblo "Indians: (Moors) have used it for years to make childbirth easier. If the baby is ready to be born, it will help dilate the cervix.

Caution: large doses could cause headache, thirst or convulsions. Activated charcoal will help counteract any negative effects.

Brigham tea (ephedra nevadensis) (herb):

Arthritis, asthma, blood pressure, blood pressure, blood purifier, childhood diseases, colds, fever, hay fever, headache, kidneys, menstruation, nosebleed, rheumatism, sinus congestion, skin problems

This herb is an excellent spring tonic. It contains ephedrine (adrenalin), which stimulates the sympathetic nervous system which may cause nervousness and restlessness in some people.

Buchu (barosma crenata) (barosma betulina):

Bed wetting, bladder weakness, diabetes, gravel, pancreas, prostate gland, rheumatism, skin problems, warts, worms

Is excellent for all types of urinary disorders-including infection, irritation, urine retention, and mucous. It is more effective when taken in combination with uva ursi.

Buckthorn (rhamnus frangula) (bark):

Constipation, gall stones, gout, hemorrhoids, itching, liver, parasites, perspiration, rheumatism, skin problems, warts, worms

Buckthorn is used mainly as a laxative and is not habit forming. If nausea occurs, this indicates the body has had sufficient-discontinue its use.

Burdock (atrium lappa) (root):

Acne, allergies, arthritis, baldness, bladder, blood purifier, boils, burns, bursitis, cankers, childhood diseases, cleansing, dandruff, endurance, energy, fatigue, gall bladder, gall stones, gout, hay fever, hemorrhoids, itching, kidneys, liver, lungs, lymph glands, nervous disorders, obesity, poison ivy, psoriasis, rheumatism, skin problems, sore throat, tonsillitis, ulcers, venereal disease, vitality, water retention, wounds

Burdock is one of the best blood purifiers without causing nausea or irritation. It helps to reduce swelling and deposits in the joints in arthritis. Used internally and externally for skin problems. The burns are used for water retention. The leaves are used extremely for burns, skin problems, and wounds.

Chamomile (matricaria chamomilla) (flowers):

Appetite, asthma, bladder, bleeding, blodd purifier, bronchitis, callouses, childhood diseases, colds, colic, colitis, colon, corns, cramps, dandruff, digestive disorders, dizziness, drug withdrawal, earache, eyes, food poisoning, gas, headache, hemorrhage, hemorrhoids, inflammation, insomnia, jaundice, kidneys, menstruation, migraine headache, nervous disorders, pain, parasites, spleen, swelling, toothache, worms, wounds

Chamomile has been used very successfully as a cleaner for those who have used drugs over along period of time. The tea is good for digestive disorders and tones the complete digestive tract. It is used for expelling worms in children and also as a hair rinse to add luster to the hair. Large doses act as an emetic without depressing the system. When used externally as a poultice, it has a drawing and cooling effect. It is often used for preventing migraine headaches.

Cascara sagrada (rhamnus purshiana) (Bark):

Colon; constipation; cough; croup; digestive disorders; gall bladder; gall stones; hemorrhoids; jaundice; laxative; liver; nervous disorders; pancreas;

spleen

Cascara Sagrada is known as "Doan's Pills." It is mainly used for colon related problems. It stimulates secretions of the liver, pancreas, and stomach when taken internally. Use in small but frequent doses. In chronic constipation, gradually decrease the dose to stimulate the peristaltic action of the colon. It should be taken on an empty stomach. As it restores the tone of the bowel it produces a permanent beneficial effect. It is good taken upon retiring as it helps to relax and soothe the system.

Catnip (nepeta cataria) (herb):

Bronchitis, childhood diseases, colds, colic, convulsions, cramps, croup, diarrhea, dizziness, fever, flu, gas, headache, hypoglycemia, insomnia, kidney stones, menstruation, miscarriage, morning sickness, nervous sickness, nightmares, pain, parasites, smoking, stress, tension, uterus, water retention

Catnip is used to stop vomiting. The tea is good for colic infants. For fever, use the tea as an enema. This enema is soothing and relaxing and helps dislodge congestion in the colon. Chew the fresh leaves for toothache. Catnip elevates the mood and gives a feeling of well-being.

Cayenne (capsicum annum, capsicum frutescens) (fruit):

Acne, alcoholism, appetite, arteriosclerosis, arthritis, asthma, bleeding, blood pressure, cramps, cuts, diabetes, digestive disorders, douche, endurance, energy, eyes, fatigue, flu, fractures, gas, hay fever, heart stimulant, hemorrhage, hemorrhoids, infection, jaundice, kidneys, lungs, menstruation, migraine headache, miscarriage, pancreas, paralysis, pleurisy, rheumatism, sinus congestion, shock, spleen, sore throat, tonsillitis, ulcers, vagina, varicose veins, vitality, wounds, yeast infection

Cayenne has been recognized as one of the greatest of all herbs, not only for the entire digestive system, but for the circulatory system as well. It has been known as an excellent remedy for hemorrhoids. It helps to regulate the heart and blood pressure; it strengthens the pulse rate while it cleanses the circulatory system. When taken with ginger, it helps clean out the bronchial tubes. Used with garlic it helps lower the blood pressure. When it is used with other herbs, it acts as a catalyst and increases the effectiveness of the other herbs. It is used for those who are shock. It helps stop internal or external bleeding if taken internally, or if the wound is small. Cayenne may be applied directly to it. Extract of cayenne is especially good used as a liniment for headaches, rheumatism, and muscle aches. A small amount of powder sprinkled in your shoes in cold weather will keep your feet warm.

Chaparral (larrea divaricate, larrea Mexicana) (herb)

Acne, allergies, arthritis, asthma, baldness, blood purifier, boils, bursitis, cancer, cataracts, cleansing, cramps, dandruff, eyesight, hay fever, insomnia, kidneys, obesity, prostate gland, psoriasis, rheumatism, skin problems, tumors, warts, wounds

Chaparral is an astringent and is used externally for sores and wounds. When combined with red clover it is used to rid the body of growths and tumors by purifying the blood.

Chickweed (sterllaria media) (herb):

Acne, allergies, appetite (decrease), asthma, blood poisoning, boils, bronchitis, burns, cancer, canker, circulation, cleansing, colon, constipation, diabetes, frigidity, hay fever, hemorrhoids, hoarseness, impotence, inflammation, itching, mouth sores, obesity, pleurisy, psoriasis, rheumatism, skin problems, sore throat, sterility, swelling, tumors, ulcers, wounds

Good to stop bleeding and inflammation from lungs, bowels, and stomach. Used as a poultice for rashes and sores. High I vitamin C. Helps liquefy and remove mucous from respiratory tract. Helps dissolve fat in the body. May be used as an external scrub for acne.

Chlorophyll:

Acne, anemia, asthma, bad breath, blood purifier, body odor, cleansing, colon, deodorizer, diabetes, digestive disorders, energy, foot order, fractures, heart, hemorrhage, hemorrhoids, hypoglycemia, lactation, liver, menstrual cramps, mouth sores, sore throat, thyroid gland, tonsillitis, ulcers

Chlorophyll may betaken internally or in an enema to remove body odors. It is used as a gargle for sore throat and bad breath. Very high in trace minerals. It has a high calcium andiron content. Iron is necessary for glands to receive sufficient oxygen. It helps to replace calcium lost during menstruation. It is an excellent blood purifier. Produces some milk in nursing mothers. It is good for hemorrhages because it is high in vitamin k which helps coagulate the blood. Liquid chlorophyll aids the flow of bile, which in turn acts as an irritant to encourage the bowel to function properly.

Comfrey (Symphytum officinale) (root):

Allergies, anemia, arthritis, asthma, bladder, bleeding, blood purifier, boils, bronchitis, bruises, burns, bursitis, colds, colitis, colon, cough, cramps, diabetes, diarrhea, digestive disorders, eczema, fatigue, fractures, gall bladder, gout, gums, hsasy fever, headache, hemorrhage, hoarseness, infection, inflammation, insect bites, kidneys, laxative, leucorrhea, lumbago, lungs, menstruation, mucous membranes, pneumonia, psoriasis, rheumatism, sinus congestion, sore throat, sprains, swelling, tonsillitis, ulcers, wounds

Comfrey helps to eliminate bloody urine. It is high in potassium, vitamin A, and calcium. The allantoin in comfrey is the same ingredient contained in aloe vera. It is soothing to the gastrointestinal tract. It acts a mild laxative. Poultices of comfrey are very beneficial for wounds, sprains, sores, and inflammations. Helps to heal broken or fractured bones and is often referred to as the "bone-knitter."

Corn-silk (zea mays) (silk):

Bed wetting, bladder, bleeding, childbirth, gout, kidneys, pain, prostate gland, urinary disorders, uterine problems, water retention

Helps rid the body of the ammonia odor in the urine. It is good for chronic urinary disorders and will alleviate painful urination due to prostate gland problems. It reduces uric acid build-up. Helps uterine contractions in childbirth. It also slows down bleeding after the baby is born. It will bring the contractions back during childbirth if the labor stops,

Couch grass (agropyron repens)(herbs):

Bladder, blood purifier, bronchitis, constipation, kidneys, gout, gall stones, gravel, jaundice, liver, parasites, water retention

Promotes urination. Especially effective when taken in combination with other herbs.

Cramp bark (viburnum opulus, v. americanum) (bark):

Cramps, kidneys, menstruation, miscarriage, nervous disorders, urinary disorders

Helps prevent miscarriage. It relaxes the ovaries and uterus. Helps alleviate cramps in limbs during pregnancy. Will stimulate the kidneys. It acts as an antispasmodic to the body. Best when used with wild yam, blue cohosh, squaw vine, or skullcap.

Damiana (turnera aphrodisiaca) (leaves):

Female problems, frigidity, hormones(female), hot flashes, longevity, menopause, prostate gland, senility, sex stimulant

Is recognized as being good for females generally and helps to balance female hormones. It also helps to stimulate the pelvic organs. Increases the sex desire.

Dandelion (taraxacum officianle) (root):

Acne, age spots, anemia, appetite, bladder, blood pressure, blood purifier, boils, bronchitis, cancer, cleansing, constipation, cramps, diabetes, digestive disorders, eczema, endurance, energy, fatigue, fever, flu, fractures, gall bladder, gall stones, gout, heartburn, hemorrhage, hypoglycemia, insomnia, jaundice, kidneys, liver, pancreas, psoriasis, senility, skin problems, spleen, tonsillitis, vitality, water retention, wounds

Acts as a tonic to the system. It destroys acids in the blood. Contains organic sodium and is very good for anemia caused by a deficiency of nutritive salts and is recognized as a great blood builder and purifier. It is also effective as a liver cleanser. It is very high in calcium and other nutrients. It is a gentle laxative and can therefore be used in tea for babies and children.

Don Quai (angelica sinensis) (root):

Anemia, blood clots, blood pressure, blood purifier, bruises, cleansing, convulsions, cramps, endurance, energy, fatigue, female problems, hormones (female), hot flashes, hypoglycemia, insomnia, laxative, longevity, lumbago, menstrual cramps, menopause, nervous disorders, skin problems, vitality

This herb is used for almost every female problem. Helps backache caused by menstrual cramps, menopause, nervous disorders, skin problems, vitality.

Acts as a mild laxative as it lubricates the intestines. Has been helpful in eliminating dry skin problems by moistening and softening the skin. Helps to dissolve blood clots. Gives nourishment to the brain cells. High in vitamin E, B12.

Caution: not recommended during pregnancy. Could cause enlargement of the breasts.

Echinacea (echinacea angustifolia) (oil):

Acne, bad breath, bee stings, bladder infection, blood poisoning, blood purifier, boils, carbuncles, fever, gums, hemorrhage, infection, insect bites, lymph glands, mucous, prostate gland, smoking, tonsillitis, venereal disease, wounds

Is one of the best cleansers for the lymphatic system. Often used with myrrh.

Eucalyptus (eucalyptus globulus) (oil):

Appetite (improve), bronchitis, cancer, colon, cough, croup, fever, insect repellant, lungs, migraine headache, mucous, nausea, nervous disorders, paralysis, sinus congestion, sore throat, ulcers, uterus

Only administer in small doses. Helps to dilate capillaries for better circulation making it good herb for migraine headaches. A small amount on the tongue will help to stop nausea. It is an antiseptic which makes it good for wounds. Mix with olive oil or vitamin E and apply. Often used in combination with other herbs and essential oils. One teaspoon of the oil in 1 cup of warm water, rubbed into the skin is a powerful insect repellent. For coughs, it is as effective as Robitussin; one of the best for expelling mucous.

Eyebright (Euphrasia officinalis) (herb):

Allergies, cataracts, diabetes, digestive disorders, eye ailments, glaucoma, hay fever, vision

Eyebright has been used for all kinds of eye ailments and has been known to strengthen the eyes and improve the eyesight. The tea may be used as an eye wash or the herb may be taken internally.

False unicorn(chamaelirium luteum, helonias dioica) (root):

Diabetes, digestive, female problems, hemorrhage, liver, longevity, menstruation, miscarriage, senility, sterility, uterus (prolapsed),vagina

Helps tone the reproductive organs by strengthening the muscles of the uterus and has been used for all types of complications of pregnancy. Reduces pain in menstrual cramps.

Fennel (foeniculum vulgare) (seeds):

Appetite (normalizes), bed-wetting, bronchitis, colic, convulsions, cough, cramps, digestive problems, emphysema, endurance, energy, eye wash, fatigue, gall bladder, gas, gout, hoarseness, insect bites, jaundice, lactation, liver, menstruation, migraine headaches, morning sickness, mucous, nausea, nervous disorders, obesity, rheumatism, sinus congestion, vitality, water retention

Was used in olden times to improve eyesight. It is used in a tea for colic in babies. It normalizes the appetite....increases or decreases as needed. Fennel helps to increase milk for nursing mothers.

Fenugreek (trigonella foenum graecum) (seeds):

Allergies, anemia, bronchitis, bruises, colds, colitis, colon, diabetes, digestive disorders, douche, emphysema, eyes, fever, flu, frigidity, hay fever, headache, heartburn, hoarseness, lungs, migraine headaches, mucous membranes, pneumonia, sinus congestion, sore throat, ulcers, vagina, water retention

Is an intestinal lubricant and is healing for sores and ulcers in the stomach and intestines. Used as a poultice for wounds and inflammations. Helps expel mucous from the sinuses and prevents migraine headaches.

Garlic (allium sativum) (bulb):

Appetite (improve), arteriosclerosis, bee stings, blood pressure, bronchitis, cancer, childhood disease, circulation, colds, colitis, cough, cramps, croup, diaper rash, diarrhea, digestive disorders, douche, emphysema, fever, gas, heart, infection, insect bites, liver, migraine headaches, nasal passages, parasites, prostate gland, rheumatism, ringworm, sinus congestion, sore throat, ulcers, vagina, warts, yeast infection

The antibiotic action of garlic is very similar to penicillin and just as effective if taken in large enough doses, but only the harmful bacteria are destroyed. Cleanses cholesterol from the blood steam. It stimulates the digestive tract. Used to kill various kinds of worms and parasites when taken as an enema or internally. For chronic bronchitis, use either garlic or onion poultices on the chest. For yeast infection blend 1 clove of garlic in1 pint of water, strain, add one or more pints of water as a douche. Capsuled garlic can be used (2 capsules t1 pint of water). Is especially good when used with hawthorn and cayenne. In combination with cayenne it lowers the blood pressure.

Garlic (zingiber officainale) (root):

Bronchitis, childhood diseases, colds, colitis, colon spasms, cough, cramps, croup, diarrhea, digestive disorders, douche, endurance, energy, fatigue, flu, gas, headache, hemorrhage, lungs, menstruation, morning sickness, nausea, nervous disorders, paralysis, perspiration (produce), pneumonia, shock, sinus congestion, stomach spasms, toothache, vagina, vitality, vomiting (prevents)

Is used as an antacid because it blocks the breakdown of pepsinogen to pepsin-pepsin irritates the tissues and causes peptic ulcers. Add 3 or 4 tablespoons to bath water and it will help rid the body of waste and toxins by opening the pores. Ginger is especially good for colon gas when taken before each meal. It acts as a catalyst to the pelvic are.

Ginseng (panax quinquefolium) (root):

Age spots, appetite (improve), asthma, blood pressure, cancer, colds, constipation, convulsions, cough, digestive disorders, drug withdrawal, endurance, energy, fatigue, fever, frigidity, gas, hormones (balance), hemorrhage, impotence, inflammation, longevity, lungs, menstruation, pituitary gland, prostate gland, senility, sex stimulant, vitality, whooping cough

Strengthens the endocrine glands which include the metabolism of vitamins and minerals. It builds vitality and resistance. It contains steroids similar to estrogen. Ginseng helps to regulate the male hormones when used with sarsaparilla. According to studies done in Russia, the high level of physical, spiritual, emotional, and mental endurance has been attributed to the widespread use of ginseng.

Golden seal (hydrastis canadensis) (root):

Allergies, appetite (improve), asthma, bad breath, bladder, bronchitis, burns, cancer, cankers, childhood diseases, circulation, colds, colitis, diabetes, digestive disorders, douche, eye wash, flu, gall bladder, hay fever, hemorrhage, hemorrhoids, hoarseness, infection, inflammation, itching, kidneys, leucorrhea, liver, lymph nodes, menstruation, morning sickness, mouth sores, mucous membranes, nasal passages, nausea, nervous disorders, nosebleed, obesity, pancreas, prostate gland, psoriasis, ringworm, sinus congestion,, skin problems, sore throat, spleen, thyroid, ulcers, uterine problems, uterus, vagina, venereal disease, water retention, wounds

Its antibiotic action is similar to teracycline andstreptomycin. Contains hydrastine which is the same ingredient contained in visine. If a person has hypoglycemia, it is advisable to take licorice root when taking golden seal. Myrrh may be used in place of golden seal.

Gotu kola (hydrocolyte asiatica) (herbs):

Aging, blood pressure, brain food, endurance, energy, fatigue, longevity, memory, menopause, mental fatigue, pituitary gland, senility, skin problems, vitality, water retention

Is known as the "brain food" as it improves the memory and retards the aging process.it is especially good when taken with ginseng.

Hawthorn (crataegous oxyacanthus) (berries):

Adrenal glands, angina, arteriosclerosis, arthritis, blood pressure, circulation, emotional stress, endurance, energy, fatigue, heart, hypoglycemia, insomnia, kidneys, menopause, miscarriage, nervous disorders, poultice, rheumatism, vitality, water retention,

Regulates both high and low blood pressure. It strengthens the muscle and nerve to the heart. Helps prevent miscarriage. The fruit has good drawing properties as a poultice. Hawthorn may cause dizziness if taken in large doses.

Hops (humulus lupulus) (flower):

Anemia, appetite, bed wetting, cough, digestive disorders, earache, fever, headache, hoarseness, insomnia, jaundice, liver, menstrual cramps, morning sickness, nervous disorders, nightmares, night sweats, obesity, parasites, rheumatism, sex depressant, toothache, ulcers, water retention

Is a tonic and has a calming effect on the heart and nervous system. Slows down the sex desire. Contains lupulin which is a sedative and hypnotic drug. Use externally for rheumatism, bruises, colic, and skin rashes.

Horseradish (cochlerea Armoracia) (root):

Appetite (improve), asthma, bladder, circulation, cough, diabetes, digestive disorders, gas, gout, hoarseness, hypoglycemia, inflammation, liver, lungs, mucous, parasites, rheumatism, sinus congestion, skin problems, spleen, tumors, water retention, wounds.

Promotes digestion. Externally it can be applied to wounds, old sores, swelling, & tumors as a poultice. High in vitamin content. Helps reduce hoarseness in the larynx. When mixed with vinegar, it can be applied to the skin to remove freckles. Good for swollen liver and spleen. To clear nasal passages in nursing babies, the fresh herb may be held close to the nose.

Horsetail (equsetum arvense) (herb):

Baldness, bed wetting, bladder, convulsions, diabetes, earache, eyes, feet, fingernails, fractures, hair, heart, hemorrhage, jaundice, liver, lungs, menstruation, mucous, nervous disorders, nosebleed, obesity, perspiration odor, toothache, ulcers, urinary disorders, uterus, vagina, water retention, wounds.

Very healing to the stomach and intestinal ulcers because of its astringent actions. Tea is used as douche. Strengthens the hair, fingernails, and teeth enamel, it has a high silica content which helps the body to assimilate calcium.

Hyssop (hyssopus officinale) (herb):

Asthma, bee stings, bladder, blood pressure, blood purifier, bruises, burns, childhood diseases, circulation, colon, convulsions, cough, diarrhea, digestive disorders, ears, eyes, gallbladder, gall stones, gas, hoarseness, inflammation, insect bites, kidneys, lice, liver, lungs, mucous, nervous disorders, night sweats, parasites, perspiration, sinus congestion, skin problems, sore throat, toothache, ulcers

The bible tells us "Purge me with hyssop and I shall be clean." It expels mucous from all parts of the body. Use the tea as a gargle for sore throat. Regulates both high and low blood pressure. Can be used as a poultice on bruises. For toothache, boil the herb in vinegar and rinse the mouth. The mold that produces penicillin grows on hyssop leaves.

Irish Moss (chondrus crispus) (plant):

Bad breath, cancer, cough, fractures, goiter, jaundice, obesity, pneumonia, thyroid.

Because of the high iodine content, it is especially good for the thyroid. Good for respiratory tract.

Juniper (juniperus communis) (berries):

Adrenal glands, allergies, appetite (improve), arteriosclerosis, arthritis, baldness, bed wetting, bee stings, bladder, blood, boils, bronchitis, cough, diabetes, diuretic, gas, hay fever, hypoglycemia, insect bites, kidneys, lumbago, mucous, pancreas, prostate gland, sore throat, urinary disorders, water retention

Helps dilate the bronchial tubes-it is an antiseptic. Are especially helpful in urinary problems. One of the best diuretics known. Can be used as a disinfectant. Excellent for prevention of disease. Tea of the berries can be used on insect bites & bee stings.

Kelp (macrosytic pyifere) (plant):

Adrenal glands, anemia, arteriosclerosis, bursitis, childbirth, colitis, cramps, diabetes, eczema, fractures, goiter, hot flashes, hypoglycemia, kidneys, menopause, morning sickness, nausea, obesity, pituitary gland, pregnancy, prostate gland, psoriasis, skin problems, thyroid, weight distribution

Especially good for the adrenal glands. As it is a natural iodine, it helps to take weight off the hip area. Repeated small doses will decrease breast milk in nursing mothers.

Caution: if kelp is not needed, headaches could occur. Often it can be tolerated when taken in combination with other herbs.

Licorice (glycyrrhiza glabra) (root):

Addison's disease, adrenal glands, age spots, arthritis, asthma, blood purifier, bronchitis, colds, constipation, cough, drug withdrawal, emphysema, endurance, energy, female problems, hoarseness, hypoglycemia, laryngitis, longevity, lungs, menopause, mucous membranes, pancreas, pneumonia, senility, sex stimulant, sore throat, tonic, ulcers, vitality.

The tea is used for laryngitis and will restore the voice. It is also good for a mild laxative for babies. Licorice helps expel mucous from respiratory tract. It contains estroil, an estrogen. It contains nutritive and laxative properties. Licorice depresses the pituitary. It is 50X sweeter than sucrose and can be used to disguise the taste of bitter herbs. It is one of the most active herbs.

Caution: taken over along period of time, or in large doses, it can cause sodium and water retention which elevates the blood pressure and may cause pains in the heart. Listen to your body.

Lobelia (lobelia inflata) (herb):

Allergies, arthritis, asthma, boils, bronchitis, bruises, bursitis, childhood diseases, cleansing, congestion, convulsions, cough, croup, digestive disorders, ear infection, fever, food poisoning, hay fever, headache, heart palpitations, hoarseness, hyperactivity, hypoglycemia, insect bites, insomnia, jaundice, liver, lungs, migraine headaches, miscarriage, mucous membranes, nervous disorders, pain, pleurisy, pneumonia, poison ivy, poultice, relaxant, rheumatism, ringworm, shock, teething, toothache, wounds.

Is the most powerful relaxant of all herbs. It should be taken with a stimulant herb such as cayenne or peppermint. Lobeline, is an alkaloid and is the only active ingredient in lobelia. Because of the lobeline's cross tolerance to nicotine, smokers may require more lobelia. It increases the heart rate, pituitary function, the respirations and peristaltic movement.

Small doses act as a stimulant. Large doses act as a relaxant. Too much of this herb will cause vomiting.

Use the extract as a rub for relaxing a fretful baby....apply on spine. Tincture or extract of lobelia is used croup, asthma, earache, lock jaw, and ringworm.

Mandrake (podophyllum peltatum) (root):

Colitis, constipation, fever, gallbladder, gallstone, jaundice, laxative, liver, warts.

This herb is very strong and is best used with other herbs in combination.

Caution: use in small amount.

Marshmallow (althea offinalis) (root):

Allergies, asthma, bed wetting, bladder, bleeding (urinary), burns, cough, diabetes, diarrhea, douche, emphysema, eye wash, flu, hay fever, hemorrhage, hoarseness, hypoglycemia, inflammation, kidneys, lactation, laryngitis, lungs, menstruation, mucous membranes, nervous disorders, pain, pneumonia, sore throat, urinary disorders, vagina.

Because of its mucilaginous properties, it is very soothing and healing. Beneficial in removing stones from urinary organs. Used as a poultice for sprains. To increase the flow of milk and make it richer, take as a warm tea.

Mistletoe (viscum album) (herb):

Asthma, blood pressure, convulsions, gallbladder, heart, hemorrhage, hypoglycemia, menstruation, nervous disorders.

Is used as a nervine andante-spasmodic. It will stop hemorrhage from the uterus after childbirth or miscarriage. It increases the uterine contractions. It will help expel retained placenta in childbirth.

Caution: this herb should be used with caution as it may cause abortion if taken in large doses. It is used when other herbs fail to stop hemorrhage in childbirth.

Mullein (verbascum Thapsus) (leaves):

Asthma, boils, bronchitis, bruises, bursitis, childhood diseases, colon, constipation, cough, croup, diaper rash, diarrhea, earache, eyes, fever, glands, hay fever, hemorrhage, hemorrhoids, hoarseness, insomnia, lungs, mucous membranes, nosebleed, pleurisy, pneumonia, poison ivy, sinus congestion, skin problems, sore throat, toothache, tumors, warts.

Will stop hemorrhage from bowel and lungs when taken internally. Use as a tea for asthma, diarrhea (enema), and bleeding from bowels. Boil in milk for cough and diarrhea. Take in extract or tea for bronchial problems. Apply as a poultice for swollen glands, stiff neck, and mumps. Flowers steeped in oil is a good ointment for bruises and frostbite. Apply bruised leaves for diaper rash.

Myrrh (commiphora myrrha) (gum):

Asthma, bad breath, blood purifier, boils, cankers, childbirth, colitis, colon, cough, cuts, digestive disorders, douche, gums, hypoglycemia, infection, leucorrhea, lungs, menstrual cramps, mouth sores, mucous, nervous disorders, shock, sore throat, teeth (stained), thrush, thyroid (low), toothache, ulcers, vagina, wounds

It is an antiseptic which makes it good for sores and wounds. For throat and mouth sores, use as a gargle and mouthwash. Extract is used for inflamed gums, canker and thrush. Taken internally helps bad breath. Helps to prevent or clear up infection. In emergency childbirth, it can be applied to the navel after the cord is removed. It is used in place of golden seal for those with hypoglycemia.

Nettle (urtica doica) (leaves):

Asthma, baldness, bleeding, dandruff, diarrhea, hemorrhage, insect bites, kidneys, leucorrhea, lymph glands, night sweats, urinary problems

Helps expel gravel and stones from any organ where formed-especially the kidneys.

Oat straw (avena sativa) (stems):

Appetite (improve), arthritis, bed wetting, bladder, boils, bursitis, eyes, fingernails, gallbladder, gout, hair, heart, jaundice, kidneys, liver, lumbago, lungs, nervous disorders, pancreas, paralysis, rheumatism

Is very high in silica and helps the body assimilate calcium. It is especially good when used with other herbs. It helps to build strong fingernails and eliminates split ends of the hair.

Papaya (carica papaya) (fruit):

Allergies, colitis, digestive disorders, gas, liver, mucous membranes, parasites, worms, wounds

Contains papain which is an enzyme similar to pepsin-one produced by the stomach. Papaya can be mixed with cows milk to resemble breast milk. It has one of the highest enzyme contents of any herb.

Parsley (Petroselinum sativum) (leaves):

Allergies, appetite (improve), arthritis, asthma, bad breath, bedwetting, bee stings, blood pressure, bruises, cancer, cough, digestive disorders, eyes, fever, fractures, gallbladder, gallstones, gout, hay fever, insect bites, kidneys, lactation, liver, lumbago, menstrual cramps, pituitary gland, prostate gland, spleen, thyroid, water retention

Helps arthritic pain because of the high nutritive value. Will bring down a fever. Parsley will dry up mother's milk after childbirth. Bruised leaves steeped in vinegar and worn next to the breasts. Parsley helps take away odors on breath from garlic or other strong herbs. One of the best diuretics

Passionflower (passiflora incarnata) (herb):

Alcoholism, blood pressure, convulsions, fever, headache, hot flashes, insomnia, menopause, nervous disorders

When headaches are caused by nervous conditions, this herb will help. In asthma caused by stress, passionflower is very beneficial.

Peach (prunus persica) (bark):

Bladder, insomnia, laxative, morning sickness, nausea, nervous disorders, vomiting, water retention, wounds

For these conditions, the leaves are used. Peach is best used for a diuretic and a mild laxative.

Pennyroyal (hedeoma pulegiodes) (herb):

Burns, childbirth, colds, convulsions, cramps, gout, headache, itching, lungs, menstruation, mucous, nervous disorders, skin problems, sore throat, toothache, ulcers, uterus.

Used as poultice on burns. Works on uterine muscle to promote contractions. Contains an oil which relieves headaches if inhaled.

Caution: should not be taken during early pregnancy as it may cause abortion. At the end of pregnancy, however, it may be used in combination with other herbs to make delivery easier. See formula #6. It may cause nausea, vomiting, insomnia, disturbed vision if taken in large doses.

Peppermint (mentha piperita) (leaves):

Appetite (promotes), bronchitis, childhood diseases, colds, colic, colitis, cough, cramps (stomach), diarrhea, digestive disorders, dizziness, fever, flu, gallbladder, gas, headache, heartburn, heart palpitations, insomnia, itching, liver, menstrual cramps, migraine headaches, morning sickness, muscle spasms, nausea, nervous disorders, nightmares, pain, smoking.

Use in a tea form for all digestive disorders. Also, in tea for enemas. Especially good for the nervous system. Acts as a mild sedative if taken before going to bed. Use in bath for itching skin.

Plantain (plantago major) (leaves):

Bee stings, bed wetting, bladder, bleeding, blood poisoning, burns, diarrhea, douche, eyes, fractures, frigidity, hemorrhage, hemorrhoids, hoarseness, insect bites, itching, kidneys, leucorrhea, lumbago, lungs, menstruation, poison ivy, thrush, tumors, ulcers, vagina, wounds.

Is used as a poultice on all kinds of skin ailments. Rub directly on rashes caused by stinging nettle, poison ivy-oak. Used for bites, burns, rashes, poisonous spiders, and snake bites.

Pleurisy root (asclepias tuberosa) (root):

Arthritis, asthma, bronchitis, childhood diseases, circulation, cough, flu, lungs, mucous, perspiration, pleurisy, rheumatism, pneumonia, tonsillitis, water retention

Is used to relax the capillaries. It is used in all lung-related problems.

Caution: do not use when skin is cold, and pulse is weak.

Poke weed (phytolacca decandra) (root)

Breasts, cancer, constipation, goiter, gums, hemorrhoids, infection, inflammation, laxative, liver, lumbago, lymph glands, pain, parasites, rheumatism, ringworm, skin problems, thyroid, tumors, ulcers

For inflamed or swollen breasts, use internally or as a poultice. Regulates the thyroid gland. Should be used in small doses.

Caution: may cause digestive upset.

Primrose (primula vulgaris, p. officaianalis) (seed, oil):

Arthritis, blood pressure, bronchitis, convulsions, gallstones, gout, insomnia, nervous disorders, pain, rheumatism, stomach, toothache

Acts as a stimulant to the bronchial tubes and stomach. It is an antispasmodic. It neutralizes over-acidity in the body. The root is used to expel worms. Best used in an oil.

Psyllium (plantago psyllium) (seed):

Colitis, colon, constipation, laxative, hemorrhoids, ulcers

Helps to lubricate and heal the intestinal tract. It also moistens and acts as a bulk agent. It is sold in stores under the name Metamucil.

Queen of the meadow (eupatorium purpureum) (leaves):

Diabetes, gout, kidneys, lumbago, nervous disorders, prostate gland, rheumatism, stones, urinary disorders, psoriasis, rheumatism, skin problems, tumors.

This herb has been used to restore fertility. It is a mild laxative. Especially good to calm the nerves and cleanse the blood. It helps to break up growths and tumors when used in combination with chaparral and other herbs.

Red clover (trifolum pretense) (flowers):

Acne, arthritis, blood purifier, boils, bronchitis, cancer, childhood diseases, cleansing, flu, insomnia, nervous disorders, psoriasis, rheumatism, skin problems, tumors

This herb has been used to restore fertility. It is a mild laxative. Especially good to calm the nerves and cleanse the blood. It helps to break up growths and tumors when used in combination with chaparral and other herbs.

Red raspberry (rubus idaeus) (leaves):

Afterpain, bronchitis, canker, childbirth, childbirth, childhood diseases, colds, constipation, diabetes, diarrhea, digestive disorders, eyewash, female organs, flu, fractures, lactation, leucorrhea, menstruation cramps, morning sickness, mouth sores, mucous membranes, nausea, nervous disorders, pregnancy, rheumatism, sore throat, ulcers, uterus

It strengthens the uterus and entire reproductive system therefore; it is good to use during the whole pregnancy. Coordinates uterine contractions in childbirth. It is not a pain-killer-this enables it to cross the placental membrane without depressing the respiratory and circulatory centers in the brain. Decreases chance of miscarriage for premature babies. Helps mother carry baby full term as it decreases contractions in the 2nd trimester of pregnancy. For flu and diarrhea in children, take as a tea or use as an enema.

Redmond clay (montmorillonite) (clay):

Acne, bee stings, skin problems

Used as poultice to draw infection from the body. Excellent used in an enema to draw toxins from the colon. Can be used externally as a poultice for skin problems.

Rose hips (rosa canina) (fruit):

Arteriosclerosis, bee stings, bruises, childhood diseases, circulation, colds, emphysema, fever, flu, heart, infection, insect bites, jaundice, kidneys, poison ivy, sinus congestion, sore throat, tonsillitis

Excellent source of natural vitamin C. Used for infection and cleansing toxins from the body.

Safflower (carthamus tinctorius) (flower):

Appetite (improve), arthritis, bronchitis, childhood diseases, cramps, digestive disorders, fever, frigidity, gallbladder, gas, gout, heart, heartburn, hemorrhoids, hypoglycemia, liver, menstruation, perspiration, psoriasis, sex stimulant, uric acid, water retention

Prevents and helps to eliminate the buildup of uric and lactic acid in the body which causes gout. It alleviates fatigue and muscle cramps after exertion or exercise, especially in those with hypoglycemia. It is similar to chamomile in action and uses.

Sage (salvia officinalis) (leaves):

Baldness, bleeding, bronchitis, dandruff, diarrhea, digestive disorders, dizziness, fever, flu, gas, hair, headache, hoarseness, insect bites, lactation, laryngitis, lungs, menstruation, morning sickness, mouth sores, mucous membranes, nausea, nervous disorders, night sweats, parasites, sex depressant, skin problems, sore throat, tonsillitis, ulcers, worms, wounds

Contains a volatile oil and is used by dentists to decrease saliva. Tea used as a mouth wash and gargle. Helps to eliminate spasms of the gastrointestinal tract. Sage is used to help dry up milk in nursing mothers. Helps rid the body of worms in children.

Sarsaparilla (smilax officinalis) (root):

Acne, age spots, blood purifier, boils, colds, cough, eyes, fever, frigidity, gout, hormones, heart burn, hot flashes, longevity, menopause, mucous, psoriasis, rheumatism, ringworm, senility, sterility, water retention.

Contains hormones for both male and female. When it is used with ginseng, it helps to eliminate acne due to hormone imbalance in teenage boys.

Saw palmetto (serenoa serrulate) (fruit): alcoholism, asthma, bladder, breasts, bronchitis, colds, diabetes, frigidity, glands (swollen), hormones, obesity, prostate gland

Contains the enzyme lipase, which helps break down fat. It helps underweight people to gain weight. It also has been used to help increase the size of small breasts. It acts as a regular of weight and also hormones.

Skullcap (scutellaria lateriflora) (herb):

Alcoholism, bedwetting, blood pressure, childhood diseases, convulsions, digestive disorders, headache, hypoglycemia, insect bites, insomnia, nervous disorders, paralysis, rheumatism, sex depressant, smoking

Since it is an antispasmodic, it is one of the mot effective nervous system relaxants. It decreases sex desire.

Spearmint (mentha viridis) (leaves):

This herb is used the same as peppermint but because it is a milder herb, it is often preferred for small children. Slippery elm (ulmus fulva) (bark): asthma, bladder, boils, bronchitis, burns, cancer, colitis, colon, constipation, cramps, cough, diaper rash, diarrhea, digestive disorders, douche, eczema, eyes, flu, fractures, hemorrhage, hemorrhoids, hoarseness, inflammation, leucorrhea, lumbago, lungs, mucous membranes, ovaries, pleurisy, sex stimulant, smoking, sore throat, stomach, tapeworms, tonsillitis, ulcers, uterus, vagina, water retention, wounds

Can be used internally, or externally. Because of its mucilage properties it coats the digestive tract and aids in healing inflammation and is very soothing for ulcers. Blend 1 teaspoon of powder in ½ cup water and give orally in an enema for diarrhea and nausea. It can be used as a bolus for uterine problems. Excellent used as a poultice and is often mixed with golden seal and comfrey.

Squaw vine (mitchella repens) (herb):

Is an astringent, tonic, and diuretic. It works especially well for childbirth when combined with red raspberry.

Is an astringent, tonic, and diuretic. It works especially well for childbirth when combined with red raspberry.

St. Johnswort (hypericum perforatum) (herb):

Afterpain, anemia, bedwetting, bruises, burns, cough, diarrhea, gout, heart, hemorrhage, insect bites, jaundice, lungs, menstruation, nervous disorders, skin problems, ulcers, urinary disorders, water retention, worms, wounds

Used for persistent mucous problems from lungs, bowels, and urinary tract. Use as poultice for relief of local pains and bruises. Helps alleviate afterpain in childbirth.

Strawberry (fragaria vesca) (leaves):

Anemia, appetite (improve), blood purifier, bowel problems, digestive disorders, fever, gallbladder, liver, menstrual cramps, nervous disorders, night sweats, vitality

The fruit may be used to cleanse tartar from teeth and will whiten stained teeth by leaving it on for awhile. The fruit is also good for a facial scrub. The tea of the leaves is used for eczema, sore eyes, and styes on eyelids. High in minerals.

Taheebo (tabebuia avellanedae) (inner bark):

Anemia, appetite, blood purifier, cancer, cleansing, colon, diabetes, digestive disorders, hemorrhoids, hemorrhage, herpes simplex, insomnia, kidneys, leukemia, nervous disorders, pain, prostate gland, rheumatism, ringworm, skin problems, ulcers, varicose, veins, venereal disease, water retention, wounds

High in iron. It is a detoxifier. It puts body in a defensive state to give it the energy needed to defend itself and to help resist disease. Taheebo is an "Indian" name for inner bark of red lapacho tree found in the Andes mountains. It seems to be most effective taken in tea. Especially good for pain connected with cancer.

Thyme (thymus vulgaris) (herb):

Asthma, bad breath, bronchitis, childhood diseases, cough, cramps, diarrhea, digestive disorders, eczema, fever, flu, headache, heartburn, hookworms, kidney stones, leucorrhea, liver, lungs, migraine headaches, mucous, nervous disorders, nightmares, parasites, sore thought

Helps expel mucous from digestive, respiratory and urinary tracts. Helps prevent build-up of kidney stones. Expels retained afterbirth. Used with fenugreek, it prevents migraine headaches and clears sinuses.

Turkey rhubarb (rheum palmatum) (root):

Anemia, appetite (improve), bad breath, colitis, colon, constipation, croup, headache, hemorrhoids, jaundice, laxative, liver

Because it keeps the stool soft, it helps alleviate hemorrhoids. Acts as a mild laxative.

Uva ursi (Arctostaphylos uva ursi) (leaves):

Appetite (improve), bedwetting, bladder, bronchitis, cystitis, diabetes, digestive disorders, female problems, hemorrhoids, kidneys, kidney stones, leucorrhea, liver, menstruation, mucous membranes, obesity, pancreas, prostate gland, spleen, urinary disorders, uterus, vagina, venereal disease, water retention

For chronic urinary problems, this herb can be safely used on a continuing basis and in high doses.

Valerian (valeriana officianalis) (root):

Acne, afterpain, alcoholism, blood pressure, childhood diseases, colds, convulsions, digestive disorders, epilepsy, fever, gas, heart, heartburn, hypoglycemia, insomnia, lumbago, menopause, menstruation, migraine headaches, nervous disorders, pain, paralysis, shock, smoking, ulcers, wounds

Is very relaxing to the whole system. It will stop headaches due to menopause. Has a tranquilizing effect similar to Valium.

White oak bark (quercus alba) (bark):

Acne, bladder, bruises, canker, diarrhea, douche, fever, gallbladder, goiter, hemorrhage, hemorrhoids, jaundice, kidneys, leucorrhea, liver, menstruation, mouth sores, nose, parasites, ringworm, skin problems, sore throat, teeth, thrush, tonsillitis, toothache, ulcers, urinary disorders, uterus, vagina, varicose veins, wounds, yeast infection

This herb is both an astringent and tonic. Tannic acid is the active ingredient. White oak bark is good to harden the gums prior to the fitting of false teeth. It will set loose teeth and also heal most sores in the mouth. The tea is a good douche for yeast infection. A cloth wrung out of the tea and applied directly to varicose veins helps reduce the size. The herb is used both internally and externally.

Wild yam (dioscorea villosa) (root):

Afterpain, colic, gas, menstrual cramps, morning sickness, nausea, nervous disorders, pain, stomach, ulcers, uterine pains

May be taken during pregnancy to help eliminate cramps. It relieves gas pains in the stomach. Relieves nausea. Prevents miscarriage. Has been used as a contraceptive. It contains similar properties as the "pill". Contains steroids.

Willow (salix) (bark):

Arthritis, baldness, bedwetting, burns, bursitis, convulsions, dandruff, eyes, fever, gallstones, gas, gout, gums, headache, hemorrhage, rheumatism, sex depressant, wounds.

Contains salicin which is the main ingredient in aspirin.

Wintergreen (gaultheria procumbens) (leaves-oil):

Diabetes, digestive disorders, fever, headache, heart, inflammation, leucorrhea, pain, rheumatism, skin problems, stomach, swelling, varicose veins, venereal disease, water retention

Most effective as an oil. Contains salicyclic acid and when combined with acetic acid (vinegar) has the same properties as aspirin.....making it good for pain and headaches. Small doses stimulate the stomach, heart, and respiratory systems. The tea is used for gargle for sore throat and mouth and is used in a douche for leucorrhea. The oil is used in liniments. Poultices are for boils, swellings, and inflammations. It does not contain any anti-inflammatory properties therefore it is not good for arthritis and rheumatism without combining with other herbs. Excellent when used in combination with other essential oils.

Witch hazel (hamamelis virginiana) (bark):

Cuts, douche, eyes, gums, hemorrhage, hemorrhoids, inflammation, mucous membranes, nosebleed, sinus congestion, sore throat, varicose veins, venereal disease, wounds.

Used as a mouthwash for bleeding gums and after tooth extraction. Use the tea or extract as gargle for sore throat. Use packs on eyes for bruised or inflamed eyes.

Wood betony (betonica officnalis) (herb):

Asthma, bedwetting, bladder, bronchitis, convulsions, cough, diarrhea, digestive disorders, dizziness, gout, headache, heart, heartburn, inflammation, insect bites, jaundice, kidneys, liver, migraine headache, menstruation, nervous disorders, pain, parasites, perspiration, sprains, stomach, tonsillitis, varicose veins, wounds

Especially good for headaches when taken with fenugreek and thyme. It is good to heal old sores. Relaxes the whole system.

Yarrow (achillea millefolium) (flower):

Appetite (improve), arthritis, baldness, bladder, bleeding, blood purifier, bruises, bursitis, childhood diseases, colds, colic, colon, congestion, cuts, dandruff, diabetes, diarrhea, ear infection, female problems, fever, flu, fractures, headache, hemorrhage, hemorrhoids, insomnia, jaundice, kidneys, liver, lungs, menstrual cramps, mucous membranes, nervous disorders, nervous membranes, nervous disorders, night sweats, perspiration, pleurisy, pneumonia, skin problems, sore throat, spleen, uterus, wounds

Is good for clearing mucous discharge from the bladder. Will produce perspiration by opening the pores. Reduces clotting time so it is good for bleeding if used internally. Contains steroids. Use the tea for a shampoo to help baldness.

Yellow dock (rumex crispus) (root):

Acne, anemia, bladder, blood purifier, boils, cancer, childhood diseases, cleansing, diabetes, earache, ear infection, energy, eyes, fatigue, fever, flu, fractures, gallbladder, glands, gout, inflammation, itching, liver, pancreas, pituitary gland, poison ivy, psoriasis, skin problems, spleen, tumors, ulcers, venereal disease

Acts as a natural iron in the system. Especially good as a blood purifier and body cleanser.it is helpful for ulcerated eyelids. For itching, use internally or in a bath.

Yucca (yucca baccata) (root):

Arthritis, blood purifier, bursitis, gout, inflammation, joints, rheumatism, ulcers, wounds

The southwest "Indians" use it for its cleansing and detergent properties. Excellent as a hair shampoo. Contains steroids therefore it is used to reduce inflammation from the joints.

Chapter 4: Squaring the Circle

Chief Principles of the Zoroastrian Religion:

Religion should be a living force in our life and should not be confined to a study of scriptural texts. In other words, our behavior should indicate if religion is permeating (spreading or spread throughout) on all occasions.

Religion should be like a perfume spreading sweet influence through each thought word and deed.

Each man must be good and beneficent in conduct towards all around them.

He cannot injure the interests of any man or living being.

Our speech has to be sweet and beneficial.

Goodness is Godliness and a true "God (Good) Being" should be a ministering angel to all. Th Creator is so gracious in providing our needs without any expectation of a reward. So Should we radiate goodness every moment of our life.

Always try to avoid unnecessary dissensions as he is asked to be "a bridge over a gulf dividing two sects," by seeing the underlying unity, in spite of conflicting viewpoints. He is a peacemaker and would recognize some truth in every aspect of many-sided arguments. To see another's viewpoint need great tact.

One should never force his own opinion on another, as there is freedom of conscience for each of us. "Forced conversations" are never successful or long lasting. Use your "light of reason" and then formulate your own belief.

Self-sacrifice enjoins all of us to consider the welfare of others before that of our own. We grow by giving and not by acquisitive greed. We are trustees of what we possess and should willingly share our gifts with others. Charity is a special virtue, because it is our duty to improve the lot of those, who are not so fortunate in many directions.

General Discipline:

Listening: ("*Fill the ears, listen attentively*") listening to wisdom teachings. Having achieved the qualifications of an aspirant, there is a desire to listen to the teachings, from a spiritual preceptor. There is increasing Innerstanding of the scriptures and the meaning of truth vs. untruth, real vs unreal, temporal vs. eternal. The glories of Th Creator are expounded and the mystical philosophy behind the myth is given at this stage.

Reflection: ("*To think, to ponder, to fix attention, concentration*") reflection on those teachings that have been listened to and living according to the disciplines enjoyed by the teachings is to be practiced until the wisdom teaching is fully innerstood. Reflection implies discovering, intellectually at first, the oneness behind the multiplicity of the world by engaging in intense inquiry into the nature of one's true self. Chanting the divine mantras of self.

Meditation: ("*Devote yourself to adore God's name*") the process of reflection that leads to a state in which the mind is continuously introspective. It means expansion of consciousness culminating in revelation of and identification with Th Absolute Self.

*Learn ethics and law of cause and effect-practice right action (42 laws of Maat) to purify gross impurities of the personality. Control body, speech, and thoughts.

*Practice cultivation of the higher virtues (selfless-service) to purify mind and intellect from subtle impurities.

*Devotion to Th Divine; see Maatian actions as offerings to Th Divine.

*See oneself as one with Maat, i.e. united with the cosmic order which is the transcendental supreme self.

*"Self-knowledge is the basis of all true knowledge."-Ancient Axiom

*"Salvation is accomplished through the efforts of the individual. There is no mediator between man and their salvation."-Ancient Axiom

*"Salvation is the freeing of the soul from its bodily fetters, becoming a God through knowledge and wisdom, controlling the forces of the cosmos instead of being a slave to them, subduing the lower nature and through awakening the higher self, ending the cycle of rebirth and dwelling with the neters who direct and control the great plan."-Ancient Axiom

*7 Souls of Ra:

Union with the cosmic self. Meditative Principle - "I am the self."

Transcendental awareness. Meditative principle - "Spirit and matter have the same source."

Self-control. Meditative principle - I have the power to control my own destiny."

Universal love. Meditative principle-"I love and care for others and not just myself."

Power and control over others. Meditative principle - "I will innerstand my potential to serve others."

Sexuality and creativity. Meditative principle - "I will create and harness my sexuality and create positive thoughts, feelings and impressions."

Fear and survival. Meditative Principle - "I am sustained and provided for by Th Self."

*1 John 4:4-You, dear children, are from God and have overcome them, because the one who is in you is greater than one who is in the world.

Chapter 5: Energy Cleansing
Balancing the Chakra

*What are chakras?

The word chakra means wheel in Sanskrit. It acts like a spinning vortex, that carries energy throughout the body. The chakra system is a network of nerves and glands that produce, regulate and distribute hormones throughout the body. Each chakra is connected to specific organs in our body, and serve as portals that link our physical, emotional, mental and spiritual bodies.

As such they respond to vibrational frequencies emitted by our thoughts, emotions, movements, the food we eat, the air we breathe and what surrounds us like sounds, scents, light, stones, spectrums (colors), etc. By resonance it is possible to influence their frequency and correct their imbalances.

*Signs of imbalances:

When chakras are not balanced, you know it immediately! You don't feel well! The following symptoms, either physical or emotional, are indications of a situation that needs to be addressed to get the energy flowing again.

(1) Root Chakra:

Physical: weight issues, gas, diarrhea, problems with legs, knees or feet, varicose veins, impotence, insomnia, and addictions.

Overactive: intolerance, aggressiveness, rigidity, hyperactivity and greed.

Underactive: low self-esteem, insecurities, poor focus, low libido, lack of energy, lack of coordination, loneliness and depression.

Balanced: going with the flow, feeling secure and grounded.

(2) Sacral Chakra:

Physical: cramps, kidney or gallbladder problems, urinary tract infections, sexual disorders, allergies and fertility issues.

Overactive: mood swings, hysteria, sexual addictions, seductive manipulations and guilt.

Underactive: dependency, frustration, shame, over-indulgence, depression and fear of pleasure.

Balanced: enables pleasure and relationships.

(3) Solar Plexus chakra:

Physical: food allergies, parasites, diabetes, stomach problems, ulcers, shingles, obesity, stress related skin conditions and lack of memory.

Overactive: stubbornness, dread, inability to relax, anger, and perfectionism.

Underactive: apathy, feeling of rejection, mistrust, worries and dependency.

Balanced: affirmation of self, ability to shine and take your place and joyfulness.

(4) Heart chakra:

Physical: heart attacks, shortness of breath, breast cancer, hyperventilation, immunity deficiency and high blood pressure.

Overactive: feeling attacked, selfishness, excessive secretiveness and jealousy.

Underactive: afraid of letting go, tendency to withdraw and feeling unworthy of love.

Balanced: can express kindness and love freely.

(5) Throat chakra:

Physical: sore throat, teeth and gum problems, hypo or hyper thyroid, stiff neck, laryngitis, bronchitis, asthma, sinus or ear infections and hay fever.

Overactive: hyperactivity, criticize others, over-opiniated and disrespectful.

Underactive: self-criticism, hard time articulating thoughts, cowardice and bloating.

Balanced: ability to communicate and be a man of integrity.

(6) 1st/3rd eye chakra:

Physical: brain tumor, migraines, headaches, eye related issues, deafness, dyslexia, learning disabilities and autism.

Overactive: nervousness, anxiety disorders, denial, nightmares and scattered thoughts.

Underactive: chronic tiredness, dizziness, lack of common sense and poor memory.

Balanced: clear thoughts, consciousness, wisdom and guidance.

(7) Crown Chakra:

Physical: mental illness, neuralgia, seizures, sensitivity, epilepsy, varicose veins, blood vessel problems and skin rashes.

Overactive: superiority complex, lack of empathy, light sensitivity, distrust and rigidity of beliefs.

Underactive: lack of purpose, coordination problems, depression, confusion and lack of faith.

Balanced: feeling of serenity, awareness, connection to the universe, wholeness, enlightenment.

*Path to balancing the chakras:

Requires harmonizing your physical, emotional, mental and spiritual planes.

Be active, oxygen not only feeds the body, it also feeds brain cells. Accomplishing this will give you pride, which leads you to....

Be more confident. This allows you to establish satisfying relationships and display enthusiasm that will enable you to...

Express your various strengths and feel your personal power. Gaining self-esteem opens the door to...

Loving others and feeling the warmth of compassion. This enables giving and brings...

To inquire rather than make assumptions. You are able to speak your truth with clarity, sensitivity, and certainty.

This certainty will let you surrender enough to be able to perceive the purpose of life and go beyond matter. To intuitively see the big picture.

Once you see everything circularly it brings forth a sense of communication with the rest of the universe, and a connection with the divine self.

Experiences of chakra development:

(1) I saw when the lamb opened one of the seals...a white horse; and he sat on him had a bow; and a crown was given unto him: and he went forth conquering, and to conquer.(Rev. 6:1-2)

The sacral chakra ("first seal") becomes developed at birth, when the causal body (symbolized by the rider) acquires a new personality (symbolized by the horse) for functioning in the world. The color "white" symbolizes purity, indicating that the new personality has not yet been tarnished by worldly experiences. Two gifts are given at birth: a mind ("bow") having a penetrating intelligence; and a conscience, which is registered via the "crown" chakra. The purpose of being born is to "conquer" physical plane experience and thereby grow in wisdom.

(2) When he had opened the second seal....there went out another horse that was red: and power was given to him that sat thereon to take peace from the earth, and that they should kill one another: and there was given unto him a great sword. (Rev. 6:3-4)

After the solar plexus chakra ("second seal") is developed, the being is able to experience intense emotions. The color of the horse is now red, which often represents the emotion of anger. The emotion of ambition is the "power" that enables a being to compete in the world and outdo other human beings ("kill one another"). Having intense emotions is like having "a great sword" that can be used to either dominate others or cause pain in oneself.

> *(3) When he had opened the third seal....I beheld...a black horse; and he that sat on him had a pair of balances in his hand. And I heard a voice in the midst of the four beasts say, A measure of wheat for a penny, and three measures of barley for a penny; and see thou hurt not the oil and the wine. (Rev. 6:5-6).*

After the heart chakra ("third seal") is developed, the being can be intuitively aware of the essential spiritual unity behind all physical forms. This intuition is conveyed by the inner "voice in the midst of the four beasts," the four beasts representing the fourfold personality (dense physical, etheric, emotional, and mental bodies). Consequently, the being can discern the relative value of the physical side of life (as symbolized by using a pair of balances to weigh wheat and barley) while not ignoring the spiritual side of life (as symbolized by not hurting the oil and wine). The color of the horse is now black, which is a color often worn in religious orders, indicating that the being does not overly value the superficial aspects of physical life.

> *(4) When he opened the fourth seal, I....beheld a pale horse: and his name that sat on him was death, and hell followed with him. And power was given unto them over the fourth part of the earth, to kill with sword, and with hunger, and with death, and with the beasts of the earth. (Rev. 6: 7-8)*

After the throat chakra ("fourth seal") is developed, the being can more easily use his mental body to purify his emotional nature, the latter being a "fourth part" of his fourfold personality. This emotional purification can be achieved in several ways: by using the "sword" of understanding, by starving persistent undesirable habits, by refusing to express negative feelings, and by deliberately expressing other personality aspects ("beasts of the earth") through such means as physical exercises and intellectual pursuits. The color of the horse is now pale, which is the color of a sick or dying body.

> *(5) When he had opened the fifth seal, I saw under the altar the souls of them that were slain for the word of God, and for the testimony which they*

> held: And they cried with a loud voice, saying, How long, O Lord, holy and true, dost thou not judge and avenge our blood on them that dwell on the earth? And white robes were given unto every one of them; and it was said unto them, that they should rest yet for a little season, until their fellow servants also and their brethren, that should be killed as they were, should be fulfilled. (Rev. 6:9-11)

After the brow chakra ("fifth seal") is developed, the being is able to use his casual body to express intuitive wisdom easily. The casual body ("the altar") is the storehouse for the abstracted essence ("souls") that was gained by having purified ("slain for the word of God") many negative tendencies. Thus, each impurity, after being understood, becomes valued wisdom ("white robes were given unto every one of them"). Because the being still has some remaining self-centered objectives, his mastery of the physical plane ("earth") will not be complete until his remaining selfishness is eliminated ("until their fellow servants also and their brethren, that should be killed as they were, should be fulfilled").

> (6) I beheld when he had opened the sixth seal, and lo, there was a great earthquake; and the Sun became black as sackcloth of hair, and the Moon became blood; and the stars of heaven fell unto the earth, even as a fig tree casteth her untimely figs, when she is shaken of mighty wind. And the heaven departed as a scroll when it is rolled together; and every mountain and island were moved out of their places. And the kings of the earth, and the great men, and the rich men, and the chief captains, and the mighty men, and every bondman, and every free man, hid themselves in the dens and in the rocks of the mountains; and said to the mountains and rocks, fall on us, and hide us from the face of him that sitteth on the throne, and from the wrath of the lamb: for the great day of his wrath is come; and who shall be able to stand? (Rev. 6: 12-17)

After the crown chakra ("sixth seal") is developed, the being can experience continuous self-awareness, meaning continuous detached awareness of his thoughts and feelings. Thus, he is able to reorient his life ("a great earthquake") by seeing the full truth about his remaining illusions, such as false ideals ("the sun became black, moon became as blood, stars of heaven fell, and heaven departed"); material attainments and limited concepts ("every mountain and island were moved out of their place"); and various forms of pride and vanity ("the kings of the earth, and the great men, and the rich men, and the chief captains, and the mighty men, and every bondman, and every free man, hid themselves"). As a result of his continuous self-awareness, the being can proceed to eliminate all self-centeredness from his life ("for the great day of his wrath is come").

> *(7) When he had opened the seventh seal, there was silence in heaven about the space of half an hour. And I saw the seven angels which stood before God; and to them were given seven trumpets. And another angel came and stood at the altar, having a golden censer; and there was given unto him much incense, that he should offer it with the prayers of all saints upon the golden altar which was before the throne. And the smoke of the incense, which came with the prayers of the saints, ascended up before God out of the angel's hand. And the angel took the censer, and filled it with fire of the altar, and cast it into the earth: and there were voices, and thundering, and lightning, and an earthquake. And the seven angels which had the seven trumpets prepared themselves to sound. (Rev.8:1-6)*

The basic chakra ("seventh seal") is said to be developed when the being has eliminated all self-centeredness, implying that he has found freedom from all inner conflict ("there was silence in heaven"). The being can now function as an integrated spiritual triad, casual body, and personality. Thus, his nomadic will quality ("incense") can be transmitted through his spiritual triad ("another angel"), through his evolved casual body ("all saints upon the golden altar"), and through his crown chakra ("golden censer") to activate his basic chakra ("the earth"). Next his kundalini energy can awaken ("voices, and thundering, and lightning, and an earthquake") and rise to his crown chakra, thereby energizing each of his seven major etheric chakras ("the seven angels which had the seven trumpets prepared themselves to sound"). The being has completed his mastery over the physical plane.

Chapter 6: As Above so Below
*3 Types of Man (Mind): A Cosmological Guide

People who are controlled by their emotional and sensuous being. And who only "know" what they are taught by others, and whose mental perception is limited to the external and concrete side of things. Because of this their lives are full of contradictions. I.e., they are devoid of "understanding". As this type of man has not risen above the 5th division of spirit (the sahu), counting from the bottom-we shall refer to him as "sahu man." (Inferior)

People who are able to rise above the influence of their emotional and sensuous being. And although their "knowledge" is only limited to what they are able to under/inner/overstand abstractly about the subjects that are taught them. This is due to the fact that their mental faculties are able to perceive the abstractions that underlie physical events. This enables them to avoid the contradictions (falsifies) that beset the previous type of man. As the soul qualities of this type of man (mind) originates in the ab part of man/spirit, we shall refer to him as the "ab man," (Superior)

People who are able to intuit the knowledge needed to avoid and solve all the problems that can face man. They also possess the ability to achieve such objectives (influence physical events) by manipulating their spiritual power through the use of hekau (words of power/mantras/affirmations) and visualization. As this type of man has completed his/her evolution we shall refer to him as an "Ausar". (Level/Perfect man)

Each of these 3 types of people represents a stage in man's evolution. The most important factor that determines a man's behavior is his level of consciousness. It will determine her/his level of perception, which in turn will determine what s/he knows or believes, and her/his attitude toward his/her emotions and sensual appetites.

*7 days of creation:

(1) First degree (day) Sunday/ Micha'El – ruled by the Sun and Leo.

In the beginning God created the heavens and the earth, the earth was void and empty, and darkness was the face of the deep. Then God said

"Let there be light!" And light was made. This was the work of the first day.

(2) Second degree (day) Monday/ Gabri'El – ruled by the Moon and Cancer.

On the second day was created the firmament with all its expansive beauty.

(3) Third degree (day) Tuesday/ Zama'El – ruled by Mars and Aries.

Then God commanded the earth to bring forth plants, and green trees, and flowers of many various forms and different colors.

(4) Fourth degree (day) Wednesday/ Rapha'El – ruled by Mercury, Gemini and Virgo.

On the fourth day were made the great lights the shine in the heavens: The Sun, Moon and the stars.

(5) Fifth degree (day) Thursday/ Sachi'El – ruled by Jupiter and Sagittarius.

On the fifth day the fish that are in the waters, and the birds that are in the air were created.

(6) Sixth degree (day) Friday/ Ana'El – ruled by Venus, Taurus and Libra.

The sixth day God created all manner of living creatures that are upon the earth, each in its kind. At last he said: "Let us make man in our image and likeness and let him have dominion over the whole earth. So, god formed man out of the dust or the earth, and breathed into him an immortal soul, and called him Adam; that is, taken from the earth.

(7) The seventh degree (day) Cassi'El – ruled by Saturn and Capricorn.

God saw all the things that he had made, and they were good. So, he rested on the 7th day, and blissed the 7th day and sanctioned it.

Within the "genesis" of the Helios Bibliotech (holy bible), the keys to master building. "Genesis" is from the Moorish Latin meaning: birth, origin, to become, to be born, a beginning in which something is formed, creation.

In mathematics, "genesis" means to trace out to form a line, plane, figure or solid, by motion of a point, line; therefore, geometry can be seen in the story of "genesis". This is expressed by the Moabite/Moorish symbol of Isonomi, the compass and the square with the 7th letter of the alphabet-G in the center, along with the number 7, which represents the 7 ruling angels/angles/planets, the cosmos, Elohim. The Moabite/Moorish Law-Masonry, geometry, astrology- are tools of the master builder. The compass and square is also a symbolic representation of the womb-man and son, the widow and son and the virgin and her son.

*Yoruba Cosmology:

Aries - ruled by Ogun, Yoruba God of iron, war, military, force, sports, tools, blood, hunting, surgeons, police.

Taurus - ruled by Oshun, Goddess of fertility, healing, waters, sensuality, carnal love, plants, parties, seedtime and materialism.

Gemini - ruled by the Ibeji twins, duality, doubles, yin and yang, positive and negative, magic, 2 way communication.

Cancer - ruled by Yemoja-moon Goddess, maternity, mother of the waters, Ogun river, fruitlessness, trade.

Leo - ruled by Orumilla/Oludumare, God of Ifa (destiny), analysis, predictability, authority, skill.

Virgo - ruled by Eshu-Elegba, messenger of the Orisha, speech, luck, unpredictability, uncertainty.

Libra - ruled by Oshun as Goddess of Beauty, refinement, excellence, balance, sex, artistry.

Scorpio - ruled Oya-Yansa goddess of storms, Niger river, crusader, warrior goddess, death.

Sagittarius - ruled by Obatala, father of Orisha-Yodun Gods and Goddesses, paternalism, wisdom, creative intelligence, gentility.

Capricorn - ruled by Babalu-Alye/Obaku-Aiye, taskmaster God, discipline, time, cruelty, harshness, law, restraint.

Aquarius - ruled by Shango, God of thunder, lightning, fire, dynamism, invention, power, temperament.

Pisces - ruled by Olukun, God of the seas and oceans, Neptune, Poseidon, subconscious, illusions, hallucinogenic plants and substances.

*Tarot and astrology (Signs and Planet):
"The entire universe is but one vast symbol of God."-Thomas Carlyle

Signs

- Aries – The Emperor
- Taurus – The Hierophant
- Gemini – The Lovers
- Cancer – The Chariot
- Leo – Strength
- Virgo – The Hermit
- Libra – Justice
- Scorpio – Death
- Sagittarius – Temperance
- Capricorn – The Devil
- Aquarius – The Star
- Pisces – The Moon

Planets:

- Sun – The Sun
- Moon – The High Priestess
- Mercury – The Magician
- Venus – The Empress
- Mars – The Tower
- Jupiter – The Wheel of Fortune
- Saturn – The World
- Neptune – The Hanged Man
- Uranus – The Fool
- Pluto – Judgment

DECODING YOUR COSMIC BLUEPRINT

- ☉ **Sun** – How you shine, your strengths, ego.
- ☽ **Moon** – Your inner self, needs & emotional body.
- ☿ **Mercury** – Your thoughts, mental body, communication style.
- ♀ **Venus** – Your love language & feminine energy.
- ♂ **Mars** – Your passions & masculine energy.
- ♃ **Jupiter** – Spiritual talent, growth, & opportunities.
- ♄ **Saturn** – Authority, lessons, discipline, challenges.
- ♅ **Uranus** – Your inner rebel, individuality, uniqueness.
- ♆ **Neptune** – Spirituality, magic, dreams, illusion.
- ♇ **Pluto** – Transformation, alchemy, rebirth, power.

@mystic.linz

*Emotions: the signs when angry:

- Aries - 1 million in the swear jar
- Taurus - screams in the pillow
- Gemini - goes for a walk to calm down
- Cancer- so angry they go to bed to try to rest it off
- Leo - rants to themselves
- Virgo - squeezes something really hard
- Libra - gets mad in their mind, but their face is calm
- Scorpio - punches walls
- Sagittarius - breaks glass things
- Capricorn - breaths hard and bottles up their anger
- Aquarius - has to go be alone
- Pisces - listens music to calm themselves

These are accurate when one does some adjusting and adds additional information in terms of their natal chart.

When we are angry, our initial response is based on our ascendant/rising sign.

Your sun sign is how you deal with your anger, particularly based on the situation.

Your moon sign is likely how you feel you'd like to release the anger - if you are angry enough you will eventually do it.

Know yourself. Anger is a low frequency emotion. Relax and re-channel. That Mars (aggressive) and Moon (emotional) energy toward something beneficial, and work through your anger, because it leads to stress and stress kills.

*Reflections:

- Passion reflects peace
- Pleasure reflects mysteries
- Ideas reflect truth
- Compassion reflect wisdom
- Strength reflects revolution
- Excellence reflects visions

Reflections In detail:

(1) Aries (faith; center of brain): red, kidney renal, liver

- For justice
- Obtain insight
- Informed decision
- Elicit sympathy
- Peace of mind
- To have charm & social grace
- Remove indecisiveness
- Want love

(2) Taurus (strength; loins): green, urinary, genitals

- Need to know the truth
- Obtain inner vision
- Remove doubts
- Summon passion
- Remove passion
- Elicit excitement

(3) Gemini (discrimination or judgment): yellow, nervous system, muscles, thighs, skeletal

- For understanding of facts
- Seek freedom
- Instill responsibility
- Flexibility
- Good humor
- To be believed
- See the brighter side

(4) Cancer (love): silver gray, blue, legs, knees, skin

- For honors, awards, recognition
- Remove pessimism
- Remove grudges & bad feelings
- Instill ambition
- Save money
- New position or occupation

(5) Leo (power): ankles, blood, gold

When you need to know

- For wellness aid
- Elicit sympathy
- Become independent
- To be loved by people
- Summon or remove associates

(6) Virgo (imagination) ligaments, pores, perspiratory, brown

- To keep a secret
- Open a secret
- Be understood
- For imagination
- To remember & interpret dreams
- See visions
- Communicate with another plane

(7) Libra (understanding) head, eyes, brain, mental, pink and pale green
- To begin something new
- Receive energy
- Direct quick changes
- Matters of urgency
- Need courage & confidence

(8) Scorpio (will) neck, throat, deep rust, maroon
- For money
- To stand your ground
- For calmness, patience, reliableness
- For permanency
- Possessions to come to you or to be returned

(9) Sagittarius (order): purple, nose, lungs, respiratory, arms, shoulders
- To Communicate, verbal or written
- Travel
- Flexibility
- Trickery
- Hide your feelings

(10) Capricorn (renunciation or elimination): black gray, chest, stomach, gastric digestive
- Need emotional stability
- Elicit kindness
- Want protection from harm
- Need to release clinging
- Need sensitivity
- Family problems

(11) Aquarius (zeal): blue, turquoise, heart, circulatory
- Need courage, enthusiasm, creativeness
- Need to lead a group or endeavor
- When feeling aged

(12) Pisces (life conserver): sea green, intestine, bowels, abdominal
- Hold on to money
- Power of concentration
- Remember facts & details
- Perseverance
- Figuring out problems

*What makes your zodiac happy:

- Aries-money
- Taurus-food
- Gemini-sudden plans
- Cancer-love
- Leo-spotlight
- Virgo-cleanliness
- Libra-being understood
- Scorpio-sex
- Sagittarius-travel
- Capricorn-money
- Aquarius-associates
- Pisces-visualization

*The hidden side of your Zodiac:

- Aries - never letting go
- Taurus - scandalous
- Gemini - bossy
- Cancer - detached
- Leo - melancholic
- Virgo - competitiveness
- Libra - angry
- Scorpio - naïve
- Sagittarius - insecure
- Capricorn - irresponsible
- Aquarius - sensitive
- Pisces - strict

The Cave: And they do not know the future mystery or understand ancient matters. And they do not know what is going to happen; and they will not save their souls from the future mystery.

-Dead Sea Scrolls: The prophecy of the Essenes

Now has come the last age of the song of cumae. From the renewed spirit of the ages a new order is born. Now the virgin returns, the reign of Saturn returns. Now a new generation is sent down from heaven on high.

-Virgil, forth Ecologue, Messianic prophecy of the Sibyl

*Foreword:

We are electrical, magnetic, chemical, spiritual, divine beings, who transmit and receive cosmic signals (thoughts) simultaneously (hair is the natural antennae). Often we call upon or (pray) to outside energies without knowledge of our inner self. All that is in the universe is in us. We are a specific blueprint of the cosmos. "As Above -So below".

When we call on an "angel" we are calling on an "angle" of light to do the bidding of our God-Self, to go-spell (gospel). These angles of light come from the astral plane (spiritual),we are in or on the earth plane (physical). When we call on these forces, it may help to have knowledge of and/or align ourselves to receive. (Example: We may wear the color, scent, gem, or eat the foods associated with that energy, as described in this book). These are representatives of the energies and not the energies themselves. When we become in tune with natural forces, we will not need rituals, as we will become one with the "All". There are planets that give off great spiritual guidance and energies, 12 Zodiac signs, that channel that energy, 12 houses of the Zodiac represent every aspect of our lives (In my father's house there are many mansions), 12 disciples, 12 months, 12 cellular tissue salts, etc. The math breaks down to 12x12=144,000. (Coded number of chosen ones).

As the sun, moon, and planets travel through the cosmos, they shine rays of light in various configurations, creating aspects that have an affect on the actions and reactions on earth, in spite of those who may not recognize it. This book, like the cosmos uses the art of reflection. When the Sun or planets shines in one sign or area, the 180° polar sign is exalted (much like a see-saw).

Example: Aquarius and Leo are 180° apart. They are polar reflections of each other. If you desired the attributes of Aquarius you would ask for them during the time the Moon, sun or specified planet were in Leo; as attributes of Aquarius are exalted during that time, the reverse applies to Leo, and all other signs.

This Information is designed to keep you in harmony.

Month 1:

- Duration: March 21st, April 19th
- Passive: Aries
- Active: Apostle Peter Simon
- 0-30° North
- Description: headstrong, outgoing, leader, fast mover, impulsive, quick-tempered
- Purpose: to begin something new, receive energy, direct quick changes, matters of urgency, need courage and confidence. Problems with head.
- Color: red
- Metal: iron
- Scent: honeysuckle, peppermint
- Gem: diamond
- Salt: kali phos
- Foods: onions, leeks, strong tasting foods
- Herbs/spices: caper, mustard, cayenne, chile pepper
- Exalted: Apostle 6-7
- Monthly: Moon in Libra
- Annually: Sun In Libra
- Zuudiacus: 12-1 (am or pm)

Month 2:

- Duration: April 20th, May 21st
- Passive: Taurus
- Active: Apostle Andrew
- 60° North East
- Description: stubborn, honest, persistent, good with money, likes to serve people.
- Purpose: for money, to stand your ground, calmness, patience, reliability, possessions received or returned, permanency. Throat problems.
- Color: green
- Metal: copper
- Scent: apple, rose, violet
- Gem: emerald
- Salt: nat sulph
- Foods: wheat, cereals, berry fruits, apples, pears, grapes, artichokes, asparagus, beans.
- Herbs/spices: most spices, cloves, sorrel, spearmint
- Exalted: daily: Apostle: 7-8
- Monthly: Moon in Scorpio
- Annually: Sun in Scorpio
- Zuudiacus: 1-2 (am or pm)

Month 3:

- Duration: May 21st, June 20th
- Passive: Gemini
- Active: Apostle James the Less
- 90° North East
- Description: talkative, humorous, versatile, traveler, adventurous, ability to show one emotional face and actually feel the opposite.
- Purpose: to communicate (verbally & written), when travelling, for flexibility, trickery, when you want to hide your feelings. Problems with arms, shoulder or respiratory system.
- Color: yellow
- Metal: mercury
- Scent: chestnut, lavender, lily-of-the-valley
- Gem: agate
- Salt: kali mur
- Foods: nuts, vegetables grown above the ground (except cabbage), carrots, beans, peas
- Herbs/spices: aniseed, marjoram, caraway, balm, bittersweet.
- Exalted: Daily: Apostle 8-9
- Monthly: Moon in Sagittarius
- Annually: Sun in Sagittarius

Month 4:

- Duration: June 21st, July 22nd
- Passive: Cancer
- Active: Apostle John the Beloved (Luke)
- 120° South East
- Description: kind, gentle, family, down to earth, home body, sincere, stable, intuitive, honorable, consistent, emotional, moody, protective.
- Purpose: emotional stability, home stability, family issues solved, elicit kindness, protection from harm, release clinging, sensitivity, family problems. Problems with chest.
- Color: silvery grey/blue
- Metal: silver
- Scent: lily, geranium, maple
- Gem: pearl
- Salt: calc flour
- Foods: milk, fish, fruits, vegetables with high water content, cabbage, turnip.
- Herbs/spices: saxifrage, verbena, tarragon
- Exalted: daily: Apostle: 9-10
- Monthly: Moon in Capricorn
- Annually: Sun in Capricorn
- Zuudiacus: 3-4 (am or pm)

Month 5:

- Duration: July 23rd, August 22nd
- Passive: Leo
- Active: Apostle Philip
- 150° South East
- Description: eager, loyal, youthful, fearless, generous, faithful, leader, egotistical, creative, recreational
- Purpose: need courage, need enthusiasm, need creativeness, to leader a group or endeavor, when feeling aged. Heart problems.
- Color: gold
- Metal: gold
- Scent: honey & rosemary
- Gem: ruby
- Salt: mag phos
- Foods: meat, rice, honey, crops and vines in general, vegetables, high iron content, spinach and watercress
- Herbs/spices: saffron, peppermint, rosemary, rue, walnut, laurel and bay leaf
- Exalted: daily: Apostle: 10-11
- Monthly: Moon in Aquarius
- Annually: Sun in Aquarius
- Zuudiacus: 4-5 (am or pm)

Month 6:

- Duration: august 23rd, September 22nd
- Passive: Virgo
- Active: Apostle Bartholomew
- 180° South East
- Description: meticulous, inquisitive, possesses reason, analytical, critical, tenacious, stingy, attention, to detail.
- Purpose: hold onto money, power of concentration, remember facts & details, perseverance, figuring out problems. Problems with stomach/intestines.
- Color: brown
- Metal: mercury & nickel
- Scent: buttercup, oak, forget-me-not
- Gem: sardonyx
- Salt: kali sulph
- Foods: vegetables grown underground, potatoes, carrots, and all those ruled by Gemini.
- Herbs/spices: those associated with Gemini.
- Exalted: daily: Apostle: 11-12
- Monthly: Moon in Pisces
- Annually: Sun in Pisces
- Zuudiacus: 5-6 (am or pm)

Month 7:

- Duration: September 23rd, October 22nd
- Passive: Libra
- Active: Apostle Thomas
- 210° South West
- Description: love of beauty, love of love, harmony, diplomacy, sociable, romantic, sympathetic, fussy, loves learning, morality, fairness.
- Purpose: justice, obtain insight, informed decision, elicit sympathy, peace-of-mind, to have charm and sociability, remove indecisiveness, want love. Problems with kidneys or black.
- Color: pink & pale green
- Metal: copper
- Scent: mint, strawberry, daisy
- Gem: jade, sapphire,
- Salt: nat phos
- Foods: wheat, cereals, berry fruits, apples, pears, grapes, artichoke, asparagus, dried beans
- Herbs/spices: most spices, mint, cayenne
- Exalted: Daily: Apostle: 12-1
- Monthly: Moon in Aries
- Annually: Sun in Aries
- Zuudiacus: 6-7 (am or pm)

Month 8:

- Duration: October 23rd, November 21st
- Possessive: Scorpio
- Active: Apostle Mathew (Levi)
- 240° South West
- Description: suspicious, passionate, skeptical, exciting, intense, realist, compulsive
- Purpose: need to know the truth, obtain inner visions, remove doubts, summon passion or remove passion, elicit excitement. Problems sexually/genitals.
- Color: deep rust, maroon
- Metal: steel or iron
- Scent: honeysuckle, hawthorn, geranium
- Gem: opal
- Salt: calc sulph
- Foods: strong tasting foods as with Aries; onion, cayenne, mustard, peppers, leeks, shallots
- Herbs/spices: aloes, witch hazel, catmint, those associated with Aries.
- Exalted: Daily: Apostle: 1-2
- Monthly: Moon in Taurus
- Annually: Sun in Taurus
- Zuudiacus: 7-8 (am or pm)

Month 9:

- Duration: November 22nd, December 21st
- Passive: Sagittarius
- Active: Apostle James the Great
- 270° South West
- Description: versatile, quick to understand, abrupt, accurate, clarity, firm, optimistic, jovial, irresponsible, (particularly with money)
- Purpose: for understanding of facts, seek freedom, instill responsibility with money, flexibility, good humor, to be believed, to see the bright side. Problems with thighs, upper legs, hips.
- Color: purple
- Metal: tin
- Scent: cinnamon, sage, carnation
- Gem: topaz
- Salt: silica
- Foods: bulbs, vegetables, grapefruits, limes, currants, sultanas, celery, onions, leeks, chestnuts, garlic
- Herbs/spices: sage, aniseed, cinnamon, balsam, balm, bilberry, borage, dock, mosses
- Exalted: daily: Apostle: 2-3
- Monthly: Moon in Gemini
- Annually: Sun in Gemini
- Zuudiacus: 8-9 (am or pm)

Month 10:

- Duration: December 22nd, January 19th
- Passive: Capricorn
- Active: Apostle Jude (Thaddeus)
- 300° North west
- Description: materialistic, social standing, practical, cautious, calculating, aspiring, stingy, loves awards and recognition, pessimistic
- Purpose: honors, awards, recognition, remove pessimism, remove grudges/bad feelings, instill ambition, save money, new position. Problems with knees or lower leg.
- Color: grey or black
- Metal: silver
- Scent: elm, pine
- Gem: turquoise
- Salt: calc phos
- Foods: pasta, potato, barley, beets, spinach, corn, medlar, onion, quince, starchy foods.
- Herbs/spices: comfrey, knapweed, hemlock, henbane
- Exalted: Daily: Apostle: 3-4
- Monthly: Moon in Cancer
- Annually: Sun in Cancer
- Zuudiacus: 9-10 (am or pm)

Month 11:

- Duration: January 20th, February 18th
- Passive: Aquarius
- Active : Apostle Simon
- 330° North West
- Description: generous, gentle, loving, compassionate, aiding, humanitarian, loyal, independent, loves associates, know-it-all
- Purpose: need to know, wellness aid, elicit sympathy, become independent, loved by people, summon or remove associates. Problems with ankles.

- Color: blue/turquoise
- Metal: aluminum
- Scent: orchid, elderberry
- Gem: aquamarine
- Salt: nat mur
- Foods: foods which preserve well, apples, pear, lime, citrus fruits, dried fruits, kiwi, kumquat, star fruit
- Herbs/spices: those with sharp unusual flavors, pepper, chilies
- Exalted: daily: Apostle: 4-5
- Monthly: Moon in Leo
- Annually: Sun in Leo
- Zuudiacus: 10-11 (am or pm)

Month 12:

- Duration: February 19th, March 20th
- Passive: Pisces
- Active: Apostle Judas Iscariot
- 360° North West
- Description: extreme, divine, free-willing, selfless, intuitive, psychic, kind, vague, deceptive, secrets.
- Purpose: keep a secret, open a secret, to be understood, imagination, dream to remember and interpret dreams, communicate with another plane. Problem with feet.

- Color: sea green
- Metal: platinum, tin
- Scent: lime, chicory fig
- Gem: moonstone
- Salt: ferr phos
- Foods: cucumber, pumpkin, lettuce, melons
- Herbs/spices: chicory, lime, mosses
- Exalted: daily: Apostle: 5-6
- Monthly: Moon in Virgo
- Annually: Sun in Virgo
- Zuudiacus: 11-12 (am or pm)

Now is the time to come back to nature, back to our roots, back to our mother-Mother Earth.

This is the time to know yourself and the power passed down from your ancestors. You are part of a divine plan. Your natural enemy is your own will.

May we all be blessed to stand as strong as the Oak and be as consistent as the Sun and Moon. -R.V. Bey

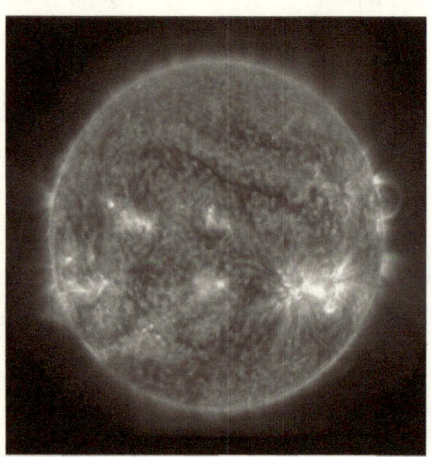

The Zodiac and the salts of salvation Pt.1: the relation of the mineral salts of the body to the signs of the Zodiac

The ancients were not "primitive men". There never was a first man, nor primitive man. Man is an eternal verity — the truth, and truth never had a beginning.

Solomon's temple is an allegory of the physical body of man and woman. Soul-of-man's temple — the house, church, Beth or temple made without sound of "saw or hammer."

The angles (angels) of the 12 zodiac signs materialize their vitalities in the human microcosm. Through the operation of chemistry, energy creating, the intelligent molecules of divine substance make the "word flesh."- Explained as God-Man: The Word Made flesh

The cosmic law is not in the least disturbed by negative statements of the ignorant individual. Those investigators of natural phenomena, who delve deeply to find truth, pay little heed to the dabbler who says, "I can't understand how the zodiacal signs can have any relation to the cell salts of the human body." The sole reason that he "cannot understand" is because he never tried to understand.

The Zodiac & Salts of Salvation
Foreword: By R.V. Bey

This booklet was written in the early 1900's, and is proof that the intentions of Modern man, over the past 100 years, (and longer) has been to suppress truths, in an effort to avow themselves as the inventors of some new ways and ideas of life. Yet, it has been written there is "nothing new under the sun". It is further proof that modern man and his modern ways have been a direct trip down a road of destruction for man and mankind. Upon research, one would find the major contributions have been weapons of mass destruction for man and mankind. Upon research, one would find the major contributions have been weapons of mass destruction. They have created unlawful statues and limitations in an effort to control people and finances that in fact violate the people's rights, in this case, to their own health upkeep. There is no mistaking that the intention was to be "God", or more accurately to be a better "God". Although all of us ought to seek our God-Self, it is clear that one ought never disobey the laws of the universe-All Law. Nor ought they disregard nature; as all beings are a product of nature, to do so is ignorance and therefore is sin.

In this foreword I have attached a drawing of the body parts of the signs of the Zodiac, so one can understand, the biochemical relationship of their bodies in an effort to begin to cure their ailments, especially in this age of mass dis-easement of people on a very personal level. The misdirecting of information and truth has led many feeling depended upon and helpless in the repair of their natural bodies, as if there are no cures, when in fact there are, and always have been. Ant suffering outside of that, would be one's "owned" fate. If this information can help those who have been stricken by ignorance and are yet willing to release themselves from their physical attachments by way of aspiring towards their spiritual connection to a oneness and wellness of themselves-so be it.

Sickness and Mental outlook:

I have found in my research that there are a lot of people who will experience difficulty in becoming well unless and until they release themselves of dishonor in their own conscious physical life, by growing spiritually conscious, and that is what science of the cell salts are about. If one feels as though they have become stricken with a diseasement, they think it is their karmic debt to be sick fort the remainder of their life. Suddenly the power of forgiveness is their own doing. Therefore, they think themselves into remaining sick. They hold themselves back by being their own judge. No man is a judge, judgment is a matter of a constant movement of the universe. You are judged as you go, and it is never to late to ask for, to accept or to be forgiven. Forgiveness is a major silent culprit, which eats at a being from the inside out.

It requires understanding, acceptance, courage and confidence. For some it is easier to remain in a fallen state, as one would not have to be responsible (respond). Their will is not willing, thereby they are the cause of their own doom. Sickness and dis-easements are a reflection of cause and effect.

There exist only 12 Bio-Chemical cellular tissue salts. They are what you may have heard referred to as "Salts of the Earth", coming from Mother Earth, and are the mineral constituents of the human body.

Physician, heal thyself!

NOTE CORRELATE CHART

NOTE	SIGN	CELL SALT	EMOTIONAL	PHYSICAL
C	Aries March 21 - April 20	Potassium Phosphate brain food; helpful for nerve and brain imbalances	Self power, ego, self direct, leader, excitement, physically motivated	Large, thick muscles, heart, gross circulation, female reproduction
C#	Taurus April 21 - May 21	Sodium Sulphate regulates the water supply in the body system	Champion of justice, fair play, hard on self, stubborn, hard on others as a cover	Tendon, ligaments, tissue linings, circulation of digestion, bowel
D	Gemini May 22 - June 21	Potassium Chloride forming and distributing fibrin throughout the body, moderates coagulation; throat, sinus	Self approval, expects reciprocation, caretaker, likes to organize, examine and fix self and others	Liver, gallbladder, pancreas, digestion, appetite, production of enzymes
D#	Cancer June 22 - July 22	Calcium Flouride muscle and ligament tonicity as well as healthy teeth enamel	Information brokers, not apt to share "real" self easily, uses narrative examples to teach	Cellular oxygenation, transport of minerals and oxygen to eyes and muscles
E	Leo July 23 - August 23	Magnesium Phosphate healthy nerve tissue, assists in nerve transmission	Self approval issues, uses words first to convey message and meaning, appreciates appreciation	Wet moist tissues, lungs, eye, nose, bronchial structures, diaphragm, mouth, gums
F	Virgo August 24 - September 22	Potassium Sulphate circulation of oils, which assists digestion and kidney function, as well as excretion of toxins through the skin	Planner, ability to see flaws in the plan of others, balance between perception and action	Kidney, environmental allergies, prostate, male reproduction, lower back, cranial balance
F#	Libra September 23 - October 22	Sodium Phosphate balances the acid-alkaline function in our bodies, helps all acid conditions which affect the nervous system	One who carries out the plans, doer, intuitive about the needs of others, shares and loves wholeheartedly	Blood filtering and screening, manages mineral balances, flow of fluids, nutrients
G	Scorpio October 23 - November 21	Calcium Sulphate good for building and sustaining epithelial tissue and all skin diseases	Game player, likes to mix and manage the physical aspects of life, motivated by future events	Neurotransmitters, balance of minerals and enzymes, bone matrix, water balance
G#	Sagittarius November 22 - December 21	Silica good for building and maintaining skin, hair, nails, and nerve coverings	Wants to make a difference, likes to help and sitisfy others, hands on, time conscious	Resource maintenance and storage, with C# retrieves nutrients from the bowel
A	Capricorn December 22 - January 20	Calcium Phosphate bone builder and helpful in any bone disease	Spiritual, takes care of the needs of others, interprets/acts from within self	Eye flexibility, electrical issues, non-physical issues, resource management, aging
A#	Aquarius January 21 - February 19	Sodium Chloride regulates the water supply throughout the body	Highly intuitive, reads between the lines, can put aside self for others, likes mental games, hurts easily	Immune system, adrenal issues with E-allergy related, body detoxification, oxygen regulation
B	Pisces February 20 - March 20	Ferrous Phosphate transports oxygen throughout the body, thus aiding circulation	Link between self and universe, needs harmony and balance in personal life and occupation	Body system integration and communication
B/C			Meditation, answers to God's LAW	Body system integration and communication

copyright © 2008 by Sharry Edwards. Original concept 1982. All rights reserved.

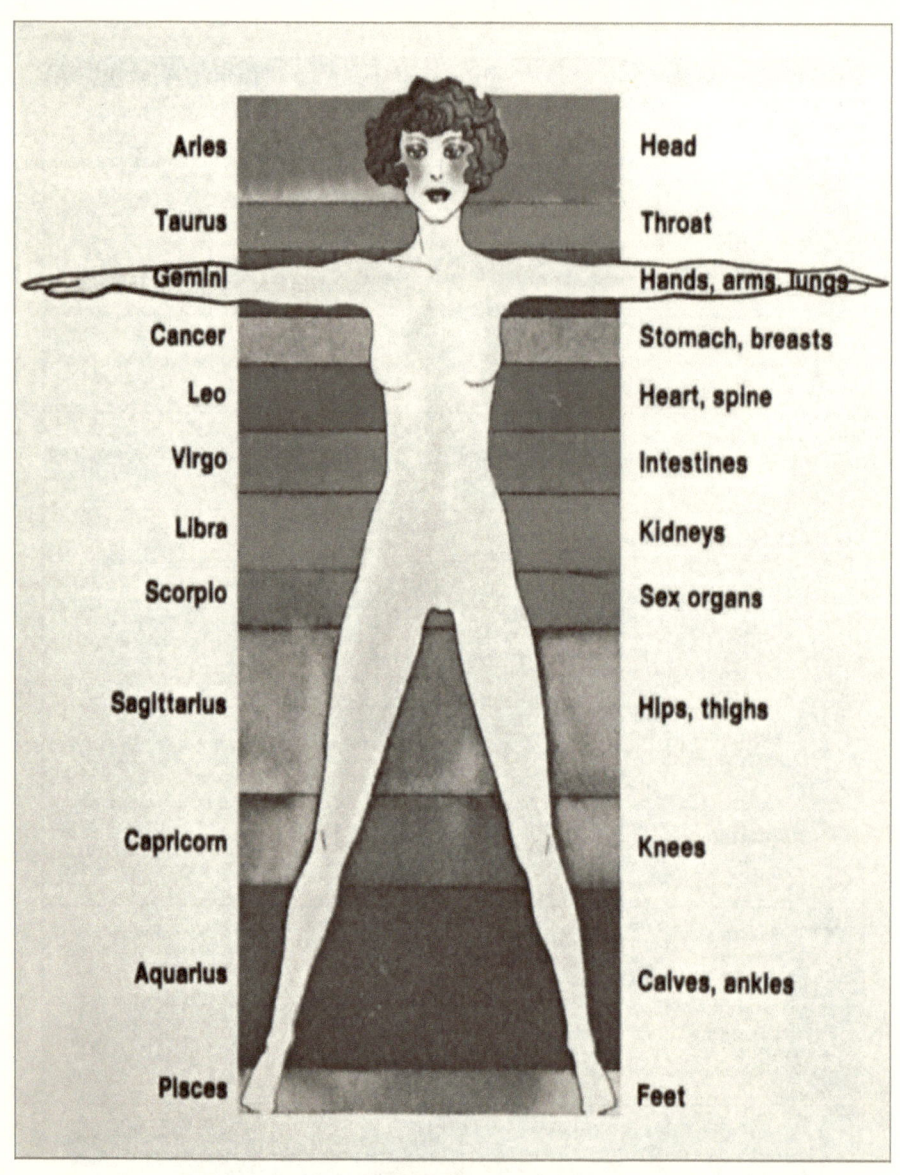

The body parts as they relate to the specific zodiac sign, which is indicative of the season of birth as it relates to the season on the earth, thereby the associated cell salt applies. Since you were in your mother's womb typically for nine months, you ought to take the cell salts of the three signs after your sign daily, like a vitamin, as you did receive any of the influences of those during your development in the womb. Therefore, your body has inherited weaknesses and the cell salts will undoubtedly strengthen you. In determining your ailment, use the art of reflection (cause & effect), as the symptom of your problem will show up in the opposite or reflected body part is indicated.

Biochemistry:

Acid and alkali acting proceeding and acting again operating, transmuting, fomenting in throes and spasms of pain-uniting, reacting, creating, like souls "passing under the rod"- some people call it chemistry, and others call it God.

Biochemistry means that chemistry of life, or the union of inorganic and organic substances whereby new compounds are formed.

In its relation to so-called disease this system uses the inorganic salts, known as Cell-salts, or tissue builders.

The constituent parts of man's body are perfect principles, namely, oxygen, hydrogen, carbon, lime, iron, potash, soda, silica, magnesia, etc. These elements, gases, etc., are perfect per se, but may be endlessly diversified in combination as may the planks, bricks or stones with which a building is to be erected.

A shadow cannot be removed by chemicals; neither can disease be removed by poison. There is nothing (no thing) to be removed in either case; but there is a deficiency to be supplied. The shadow may be removed by supplying light to the space covered by the shadow.

So symptoms, called disease, disappear or cease to manifest when the food called for is furnished.

The human body is a receptacle for a storage battery and will always run right while the chemicals are present in proper quantity and combination, as surely as an automobile will run when charged and supplied with the necessary ingredients to vibrate or cause motion.

The cell-salts are found in all our foods, and are thus carried into the blood, where they carry on the process of life, and by the law of chemical affinity keep the human form, bodily functions, ,materialized. When a deficiency occurs in any of these workers through a non-assimilation of food, poor action of liver or digestive process, dematerialization of the body commences. So disease is a deficiency in some of the chemical constituents that carry on the chemistry of life and not an entity.

Having learned that disease is not a thing, but a condition due to lack of some inorganic constituent of the blood, it follows naturally that the proper method of cure is to supply the blood with that which is lacking. In the treatment of disease, the use of anything not a constituent of the blood is unnecessary.

Dr. Chas W. Littlefield, analytical chemist, says:

"The twelve mineral salts are in a very real sense, the material basis of the organs and tissues of the body and are absolutely essential to their integrity of structure and functional activity. Experiments prove that the various tissue cells will rapidly disintegrate in the absence of the proper proportion of these salts in the circulating fluid. Whereas the maintenance of this proportion insures healthy growth and perpetual renewal.

"These mineral salts are, therefore, the physical basis of all healing. Regardless of the school employed, if these are absent from the blood and tissues no permanent cure is possible."

Osteopathy, mechano-therapy. Chiropractic, electrotherapy, naturopathy, hydropathy, massage, suggestion, mental healing, etc., are all advanced agents in keeping the human organism in perfect poise. But first of all methods, comes biochemistry to supply deficiencies in the blood. "The blood is the life", and without perfect blood, health is impossible.

Esoteric Chemistry:

In this strenuous age of reconstruction, while God's creative compounds are forming a new race in the morning of a new age, all who desire physical regeneration should strive by every means within their reach to build new tissue. Nerve fluids and brain cells, thus literally making "new bottles for the new wine": For be it known to all men that the word "wine" as used in scripture, means blood when used in connection with man. It also means the sap of trees and juice of vegetables or fruit.

The parable of turning water into wine at the marriage of Cana in Galilee is a literal statement of a process taking place every heart-beat in the human organism. Galilee means a circle of water or fluid-the circulatory system. Cana means a dividing place-the lungs. In the Greek, "A place of reeds", or cells of lungs that vibrate sound.

Biochemists' have shown that food does not form blood, but simply furnishes the mineral base by setting free the inorganic or cell salts contained in all food stuff. The organic part, oil, fibrin, albumen, etc., contained in food is burned or digested in the stomach and intestinal tract to furnish motive power to operate the human machine and draw air in the lungs, thence into arteries, i.e., air carriers.

Therefore, it is clearly proven that air (spirit) unites with the minerals and forms blood, is created every breath at the "marriage in Cana at Galilee."

Air was called water of the pure sea, viz: Virgin Mary. So, we see how water is changed into wine-blood every moment.

In the new age, we will need perfect bodies to correspond with the higher vibration, or motion of the new blood, for "old bottles (bodies) cannot contain the new wine."

Another allegorical statement typifying the same truth reads, "And I saw a new heaven and a new Earth", i.e., "a new mind and new body."

Biochemistry may well say with Walt Whitman: "To the sick lying on their backs I bring help, and to the strong, upright man I bring more needed help." To be grouchy, cross, irritable, despondent or easily discouraged, is prima facie evidence that the fluids of the stomach, liver and brain are not vibrating at normal rate, the rate that results in equilibrium or health. Health cannot be qualified, i.e., poor health or good health. There must be either health or dishealth, ease or disease. We do not say poor ease or good ease. We say ease or disease, viz., not at ease.

A sufficient amount of the cell-salts of the body, properly combined and taken as food-not simply to cure some aches pain or exudation forms blood that materializes in healthy fluids, flesh and bone tissue.

We should take the tissue cell-salts as one uses health foods, not simply to change not-health to health, but to keep the rate of blood vibration in the tone of health all the time.

The Ultimate of Biochemistry:

The microscope increases the rate of motion of the cells of the retina and we see things that were occulted to the natural rate of vibration of sight cells. Increase the rate of activity of brain cells by supplying more of the dynamic molecules of the blood known as mineral or cell-salts of lime, potash, sodium, iron, magnesia, silica, and we see mentally, truths that we could not sense at lower or natural rates of motion, although the lower rate may manifest ordinary health.

Natural man, or natural things, must be raised from the level of nature to super-natural, in order to realize new concepts that lie waiting for recognition above the solar-plexus, that is, above the animal or natural man.

The positive pole or Being must be "lifted up" from the Kingdom of Earth, animal desire below the solar-plexus, to the pineal gland which connects the cerebellum, the temple of the spiritual ego, with the optic thalmus, the third eye.

By this regenerative process millions of dormant cells of the brain are resurrected and set in operation, and then man no longer "sees through a glass darkly," but with the eye of spiritual understanding.

To those who object to linking chemistry with astrology, the writer has this to say:

The cosmic law is not in the least disturbed by negative statements of the ignorant individual. Those investigators of natural phenomena, who delve deeply to find truth, pay little heed to the dabbler who says, "I can't understand how the zodiacal signs can have any relation to the cell salts of the human body." The sole reason that he "cannot understand" is because he never tried to understand.

A little earnest, patient study will open the understanding of anyone possessed of ordinary intelligence and make plain the great truth that the universe is what the word implies, i.e., one verse.

It logically follows that all parts of one thing are susceptible to the operation of any part.

Therefore, the cell-salt corresponding with the sign of the zodiac and function of the body is consumed more rapidly than other salts and needs an extra amount to supply the deficiency caused by the Sun's influence at that particular time.

Space will only permit a brief statement of the awakening of humanity to great occult truths. However, the following from India will indicate the trend of new thought: "Dr. Carey's remarkable researches in the domain of healing art have left no stone unturned. His discovery of the Zodiacal cell-salts has added a new page in the genesis of healing art," writes Swaminatha Bomiah, M.B., Ph.D. Sc., F.L.A.C, in an article in self-culture magazine, published at No. 105 Armenian St., G.T., Madras, India.

Excerpt from George W. Carey, *Course Of Instruction In The Biochemic Pathology Of Disease*, Health Research Books, 1996.

The Twelve Cell-Salts of the Zodiac:

Aries: "The Lamb Of God"
March 20, 5 p.m., to April 20, 4 a.m.

Astrologers have for many years waited for the coming discovery of a planet to rule the head or brain of man, symbolized in the "Grand Man" of the heavens by the celestial sign of the, zodiac, regnant from March 20 to April 20. This sign is known as Aries-the Ram or Lamb.

Angles of planets cause effects or influences. The Priesthood of the middle ages, wishing to control the ignorant masses, personified the influence of planetary aspects, positions or angles, and transposed the letters so they spelled angel. Upon this one "slippery cog" the stupendous frauds of Ecclesiasticism were built.

With the false teachings of the church ingrained into the fiber of the brain of man, is it strange that for years before the advent of a new planet, with its added angle (influence), that the brain cells of Earth's inhabitants should be disturbed, as the effects of the coming storms disturb the fluids and mechanism of the weather forecaster's laboratory?

The coming of Christ and the end of the world has been preached from every street corner for several years, and thousands, yea, millions, are pledging themselves to try to live as Christ lived or according to their concept of his life.

No great movement of the people ever occurred without a scientific cause.

The optic thalamus, meaning :light of the chamber", is the inner or first (third) eye, situated in the center of the head. It connects the pineal gland and the pituitary body. The optic nerve starts from this "eye single". "If thine eye be single, thy whole body will be full of light." The optic thalamus is the Aries planet and when fully developed through physical regeneration, it lifts the initiate up from the Kingdom of Earth. Animal desire below the solar-plexus, to the pineal gland that connects the cerebellum, the temple of the spiritual ego, with the optic thalamus, the first eye. By this regenerative process millions of dormant cells of the brain are resurrected and set in operation, and then man no longer "sees through a glass darkly", but with the Eye of spiritual understanding.

I venture to predict that the planet corresponding to the optic thalamus will soon be located in the heavens.

"The order cometh."

In ancient lore Aries was known as the "Lamb of Gad", or God, which represents the head or brain. The brain controls and directs the body and mind of man. The brain itself, however, is a receiver operated upon by celestial influences or angles (angels) and must operate according to the directing force or intelligence of its source of power.

Man has been deficient in understanding because his brain receiver did not vibrate to certain subtle influences. The dynamic cells in the grey matter of the nerves were not finely attuned and did not respond–hence sin or falling short of understanding.

From the teachings of the chemistry of life we find that the basis of the brain or nerve fluid is a certain mineral salt known as potassium phosphate, kali phos.

A deficiency in this brain constituent means "sin," or a falling short of judgment or proper comprehension. With the advent of the Aries lord, God, or planet, cell-salts are rapidly coming to fore as the basis of all healing. Kali phosphate is the greatest healing agent known to man, because it is the chemical base of material expression and understanding.

The cell-salts of the human organism are now being prepared for use, while poisonous drugs are being discarded everywhere. Kali phosphate is the especial birth salt for those born between March 20 to April 20.

These people are brain workers, earnest, executive and determined-thus do they rapidly use up the brain vitalizers.

The Aries gems are amethyst and diamond.

The astral colors are white and rose pink.

In bible alchemy Aries represents Gad, the seventh son of Jacob, and means "armed and prepared"-thus it is said when in trouble or danger, "keep your head."

In the symbolism of the new testament, Aries corresponds with the disciple Thomas. Aries people are natural doubters until they figure a thing out for themselves. Aries people are natural doubters until they figure a thing for themselves.

The hour at which the sun enters a sign is figured according to Atlantic Coast time.

Taurus-The "Winged Bull" of the Zodiac:
April 20, 4 a.am., to May 21, 4 a.m.

The winged bull of Nineveh is a symbol of the great truth that substance is materialized air, and that all so-called solid substances may be resolved into air.

Taurus is an earth sign, but earth (Soul) is precipitated aerial elements. This chemical fact was known to the scientists of the Taurian age (over 4,000+

years ago); therefore, they carved the emblem of their zodiacal sign with wings.

Those born between the dates of April 20 and May 21, can descend very deep into materiality or soar "high as that heaven where Taurus wheels," as written by Edwin Markham, who is a Taurus native.

What can be finer than the following from this noted Taurian, he who has sprouted the wings of spiritual concept:

"It is a vision waiting and aware, and you must bring it down, oh, men of worth, bring down the new republic hung in air and make for it foundations on the Earth."

Air is the "raw material" for blood, and when it is drawn in, breathed in, rather, by the "Infinite Alchemist", to the blood vessels: it unites with the philosopher's stone, mineral salts, and in the human laboratory creates blood.

So, then, blood is the elixir of life, the "Ichor of the Gods."

The sulphate sodium, known to druggists as Nat. Sulph., chemically corresponds to the physical and mental characteristics of those born in the Taurus month.

Taurus is represented by the cerebellum, or lower brain, and neck.

A deficiency in Nat. Sulph. In the blood is always manifested by pains in the back of the head, sometimes extending down the spine, and then affecting the liver.

The first cell-salt to become deficient in symptoms of disease in the Taurus native is Nat Sulph.

The chief office of Nat. Sulph. Is to eliminate an excess of water from the body.

In hot weather the atmosphere becomes heavily laden with water and is thus breathed into the blood through the lungs.

One molecule of the Taurus salt has the chemical power to take up and carry out the system two molecules of water.

Blood does not become overcharged with water from the water we drink, but from an atmosphere overcharged with aqueous vapor drawn from water in rivers, lakes or swamps, by heat of the sun above 70 degrees in shade.

The more surplus water there is to be thrown out of the blood, the more sodium sulphate required.

All so-called bilious or malarial troubles are simply a chemical effect or action caused by deficient sulphate of soda.

Chills and fever are nature's method of getting rid of surplus water by squeezing it out of the blood through violent muscular, nervous and vascular spasms.

No "shakes" or ague can occur if blood be properly balanced chemically.

Governing planet: Venus.

Gems: moss-agate and emerald.

Astral colors: red and lemon yellow.

In bible alchemy Taurus represents Asher, the eighth son of Jacob, and means blessedness or happiness.

In the symbolism of the New Testament. Taurus corresponds with the disciple Thaddeus, meaning firmness, or led by love.

The chemistry of Gemini:
May 21 to June 21, Noon

One of the chief characteristics of the Gemini native is expression. The cell-salt kali muriaticum (potassium chloride) is the mineral worker of blood that forms fibrine and properly diffuses it throughout the tissues of the body.

This salt must not be confused with the chlorate of potash, a poison (chemical formulae K. CLOs).

The formulae of the chloride of potassium (kali mur) is K. CI.

Kali mur molecules are the principle agents used in the chemistry of life to build fibrine into the human organism. The skin that covers the face contains the lines and angles that give expression and thus differentiate one person from another; therefore, the maker of fibrine has been designated as the birth *salt of the Gemini native.*

In venous blood fibrine amounts to three in one thousand parts. When the molecules of kali mur fall below the standard, the blood fibrine thickens, causing what is known as pleurisy, pneumonia, catarrh, diphtheria, etc. When the circulation fails to throw out the thickened fibrine via the glands or mucous membrane, it may stop the action of the heart. Embolus is a Latin word meaning little lump, or balls; therefore, to die of embolus, or "heart failure", generally means that the heart's action was stooped by little lumps of fibrine clogging the auricles and ventricles of the heart.

When the blood contains the proper amount of kali mur, fibrine is functional and the symptoms referred to above do not manifest. Gemini is the sign which governs the "United States."

The astral colors of Gemini are red, white and blue. While those who made the banner and chose the colors personally knew nothing of astrology (supposedly), yet the cosmic law

Worked its "will to give the U.S.," which is an appendage of America, the "red, white and blue."

Mercury is the governing planet of Gemini.

The gems are beryl, aquamarine and dark blue stones.

In bible alchemy Gemini represents Issachar, the ninth son of Jacob, and means price, reward or recompense. In the symbolism, allegories of the New testament, Gemini corresponds with the disciple Judas, which means service or necessity. The perverted ideas of an ignorant dark-age priesthood made "service and necessity" infamous by a literal rendering of the alchemical symbol, but during the present Aquarian age, the Judas symbol will be understood, and the disciple of "service" will no longer have to submit to "third degree methods."

The Chemistry of the Crab:
June 21, noon, to July 22, 11 p.m.

Cancer is the mother sign of the zodiac.

The mother's breast is the soul's first home after taking on flesh and "rending the veil of Isis".

The tenacity of those born between the dates June 21 and July 22, in holding on to a hone or dwelling place is well illustrated by the crab's grip, and also by the fact that it may be sure of a dwelling.

The angles (Angels) of the twelve zodiacal signs materialize their vitalities in the human microcosm. Through the operation of chemistry, energy creating, the intelligent molecules of divine substance make the "Word flesh."

The corner stone in the chemistry of the crab is the inorganic salt fluoride of lime, known in pharmacy language as calcarea fluorica. It is a combination of fluorine and lime.

When this cell-salt is deficient in the blood, physical and mental disease (not-at-ease) is the result. Elastic fiber is formed by the union of the fluoride of lime with albuminoids, whether in the rubber tree or the human body. All relaxed conditions of tissue (varicose veins and kindred ailments) are due to lack of sufficient amount of elastic fiber to "rubber" the tissue and hold it in place.

When this cell-salt is deficient in tissue of membrane between the upper and lower brain poles cerebrum and cerebellum-there results a "sagging apart" of the positive and negative poles of the dynamo that runs the machinery of man.

An unfailing sign or symptom of this deficiency is a groundless fear or financial ruin.

While those born in any of the twelve signs may sometimes be deficient in cal. Fluoride due to Mars or Mercury (or both) in Cancer at birth, Cancer people are more liable to symptoms, indicating a lack of this elastic fiber-builder than are those born in other signs.

Why should we search Latin and Greek lexicons to find a name for the result of a deficiency in some of the mineral constituents of blood? If we find a briar in our flesh, we say so in the plainest speech; we do not say, "I have got the bursitis or splintraligia."

When we know that a deficiency in the cell salts of the blood causes symptoms that medical ignorance has dignified and personified with names that nobody knows the meaning of, we will know how to scientifically heal by the unalterable law of the chemistry of life. When we learn the cause of disease, then, and not before, will we prevent disease.

Not through quarantine, nor disinfectants nor "boards of health" will man reach the long-sought plane of health; not by dieting or fasting or "fletcherizing" or suggesting, will the elixir of life and the philosopher's stone be found.

The "Mercury of the sages" and the "hidden manna" are not constituents of health foods.

Victims of salt baths and massage are bald before time, and the alcohol, steam and Turkish bath fiends die young.

"Sic transit gloria mundi."

When a man's body is made chemically perfect, the operations of mind will perfectly express.

Gems belonging to the sign of the breast are onyx and emerald; astral colors green and russet brown.

Cancer is represented by Zebulum, the 10th son of Jacob, and means dwelling place or habitation.

Matthew is the Cancer disciple.

Leo, the heart of the zodiac:
July 22, 11 p.m., to August 23, 6 a.m.

The sun overflows with divine energy. It is the "brewpot" that forever filters and scatters the "elixir of life." Those born while the sun is passing through Leo, July 22 to August 23, receive the heart vibrations, or pulses, of the Grand Man, or "Circle of Beasts." All the blood in the body passes through the heart and the Leo native is the recipient of every quality and possibility contained in the great "Alchemical Vase", the "Son of Heaven."

The impulsive traits of Leo people are symbolled in the pulse which is a reflex of heart throbs.

The astronomer, by the unerring law of mathematics applied to space, proportion, and the so-far-discovered wheels and cogs of the uni-machine, can tell where a certain planet must be located before the telescope has verified the prediction. So the astro-biochemist knows there must of necessity be a blood mineral and tissue builder to correspond with the materialized angle (angel) of the circle of the Zodiac.

The phosphate of magnesia, in biochemic therapeutics, is the remedy for all spasmodic impulsive symptoms. It supplies the deficient worker or builder in such cases and thus restore normal conditions. A lack of muscular force or nerve vigor indicates a disturbance in the operation of the heart cell-salt, magnesia phosphate, which gives the "Lion's spring," or impulse, to the blood that throbs through the heart.

Leo is ruled by the Sun, and the children of that celestial sign are natural sun worshippers.

Gold must contain a small percent of alloy or base metal before it can be used commercially. Likewise, the "Gold of Ophir"-Sun's rays, or vibration-must contain a high potency of the earth salt, magnesia, in order to be available for use in bodily function. Thus, through the chemical action of the inorganic (mineral and water) in the organic, Sun's rays and ether, does the volatile become fixed, and the word becomes flesh.

Leo people consume their birth salts more rapidly than they consume any of the other salts of the blood; hence are often deficient in magnesium. Crude magnesia is too coarse to enter the blood through the delicate mucus membrane absorbents and must be prepared according to the biochemic method before taken to supply the blood.

Gems of Leo are ruby and diamond.

Astral colors, red and green.

The eleventh child of Jacob, Dinah, represents Leo and means Judged. Simon is the Leo disciple.

Virgo: The Virgin Mary

August 23, 6 a.m, to September 23, 3 A.M.

Virgin means pure. Mary, Marie, or Mare (Mar) means water. The letter M is simply the sign of Aquarius, "The Water Bearer."

Virgin Mary means pure sea, or water.

Jesus is derived from a Greek word, meaning fish. Out of the pure sea, or water, comes fish. Out of woman's body comes the "word made flesh". All substance comes forth from air, which is a higher potency of water.

All substance is fish, or the substance of Jesus.

This substance is made to say, "Eat, this is my body; drink, this is my blood."

There is nothing from which flesh and blood can be made, but the one universal air, energy, or spirit, in which man has his being.

All tangible elements are the effects of certain rates of motion of the intangible and unseen elements. Nitrogen gas is mineral in solution, or ultimate potency.

Oil is made by the union of the sulphate of potassium (potash), with albuminoids and aerial elements.

The first element that is disturbed in the organism of those born in the celestial sign Virgo 11 (sodium); this break in the function of oil shows a deficiency in potassium sulphate, known in pharmacy as kali sulph.

Virgo is represented in the human body by the stomach and bowels, the laboratory in which food is consumed as fuel to set free the minerals, in order that they may enter the blood through the mucous membrane absorbents.

The letter X in Hebrew is Samech or Stomach, X, or cross, means crucifixion, or change-transmutation.

Virgo people are discriminating, analytical and critical.

The microscope reveals the fact that when the body is in health little jets of stream are constantly escaping from the seven million pores on the skin. A deficiency in kali sulph molecules causes the oil in the tissue to thicken and clog these safety vales of the human engine, thus turning heat and secretions back upon the inner lungs, pleura, membrane of nasal passages, etc. And does it not seem strange that medical science, that boasts of such great progress, can invent no better term than "bad cold" for these chemical results?

Kali sulph is found in considerable quantities in the scalp and hair. When this salt falls below the standard, dandruff or eruptions, secreting yellowish, thin, oily matter or falling out of the hair is the result.

Kali sulph is a wonderful salt, and its operation in the divine laboratory of man's body, where it manufactures oil, is the miracle of the chemistry of life.

Governing planet, Mercury.

Gems, pink jasper and hyacinth.

In bible alchemy Virgo is represented by Joseph, the twelfth son of Jacob, and means: to increase power, or "Son of the Right Hand."

Virgo corresponds with the disciple Bartholomew.

Libra: The Loins
September 23, 3 A.M., to October 23, Noon

This alkaline cell-salt is made from bone ash or by neutralizing orthophosphoric acid with carbonate of sodium.

Libra is a Latin word, meaning scales or balance. Sodium, or natrum, phosphate holds the balance between acids and the normal fluids of the human body.

Acid is organic and can be chemically split into two or more elements, thus destroying the formula that makes the chemical rate of motion called acid.

A certain amount of acid is necessary and is always present in the blood, nerve, stomach and liver fluids. The apparent excess of acid is nearly always due to a deficiency in the alkaline, Libra, salt.

Acid, in alchemical lore, is represented as Satan (Saturn), while sodium phosphate symbols Christ (Venus). An absence of the Christ principles gives license to Satan to run riot in the Holy Temple. The advent of Christ drives the evil out with a whip of thongs. Reference to the temple in the figurative *language of the bible and new testament always symbols the human organism. "Know ye not that your bodies are the temple of the living God?"*

Solomon's temple is an allegory of the physical body of man and woman. Soul-of-man's temple the house, church, Beth or temple made without sound of "saw or hammer."

Hate, envy, criticism, jealousy, competition, selfishness, war, suicide and murder are largely caused by acid conditions of the blood, producing changes by chemical poisons and irritation of the brain cells, the keys upon which the soul plays "Divine Harmonies" or plays "fantastic tricks before high heaven," according to the arrangement of chemical molecules in the wondrous laboratory of the soul.

Without a proper balance of the Venus salt, the agent of peace and love, man is fit for "treason, stratagems and spoils."

The people of the world never needed the alkaline of Libra salt more than they do at the present time, while wars and rumors of wars strut upon the stage of life (1918).

The Sun enters Libra September 23 and remains until October 23.

Governing planet, Venus.

Gems, diamond and opal.

Astral colors are black, crimson and light blue. Libra is an air sign.

In bible alchemy, Libra represents Rueben, the first son of Jacob. Reuben means vision of the sun.

In the symbolism of the new testament Libra corresponds with the disciple Peter.

Peter is derived from Petra, a stone or mineral. On the ‚Peter (mineral), will I build my church, viz., Beth, house, body or temple.

Influence of Sun on vibration of blood at birth: Scorpio
October 23, noon, to November 22, 5 a.m.

From scorpion to "white eagle" may seem a very long journey to one who has not learned the science of patience or realized that time is an illusion of physical sense.

The Zodiacal sign Scorpio is represented in human material organism by the sexual functions.

The esoteric meaning of sex is based on mathematics, the body being a mathematical fact. Sex in Sanskrit means six.

"Six days of Creation" simply means that all creation, or formation, from self-existing substance, is by and through the operation of the sex principle—the only principle.

Three means male, father, the spirit of the male, and son; this trinity forms or constitutes one pole of being, energy or life—the positive pole.

The negative pole, female trinity; female spirit of mother and daughter.

Thus, two threes or trinities produce six or sex, the operation of which is the cause of all manifestation. Those who understand fully realize the truth of the new testament statement, "there is no other name under heaven whereby ye may be saved (materialized and sustained), except through Jesus and crucify (also Christ) to their roots a wonderful world of truth appears to the understanding.

The possibilities of Scorpio people are boundless after they have passed through trials and tribulations, viz: crucifixion or crossification.

One of the cell-salts of the blood, calcarea sulphate, is the mineral ("stone") that especially corresponds to the Scorpio nature. Crude Calcerea sulphate is gypsum or sulphate of lime.

While in crude form lime is of little value but add water and thus transmute it by changing its chemical formation, and plaster of Paris is formed, a substance useful and ornamental. Every being, born between October 23 and November 22, should well consider this wonderful alchemical operation of their esoteric stone and thus realize the possibilities in store for them on their journey to the "Eyrie of the White Eagle."

Scorpio people are natural magnetic healers, especially after having passed through the waters of adversity, as heat is caused by the union of water and lime.

Scorpio is a water sign, governed by Mars. Mars is "a doer of things", also fiery at times, therefore, it is well that the Scorpio native take heed lest he sometimes "boil over."

In bible alchemy, Scorpio is represented by Simeon, the second son of Jacob. Simeon means "hears and obeys." In the symbolism of the new testament Scorpio corresponds with the disciple Andrew, to create or ascend.

The gems are topaz and malachite; astral colors, golden brown and black.

A break in the molecular chain of the Scorpio salt, caused by a deficiency of that material in the blood, is the primal cause of all the so-called diseases of these people. This disturbance not only causes symptoms called disease in physical functions, but it disturbs the astral fluids and gray matter of brain cells and thereby changes the operation of mind into harmony. Sin means to lack or fall short; thus, chemical deficiencies in life's chemistry cause sin.

When man learns to supply his dynamo with the proper dynamics, he wilt "wash away his sins with the blood of Christ"-blood made with the "White Stone."

Calcium sulphate should not be taken internally in crude form; in order to be taken up by absorbents of mucous membrane the lime salt must be triturated.

According to the biochemic method up to 3rd or 6th. By this method lime may be rendered as fine as the molecules contained in grain, fruit or vegetables.

Blood contains three forms of Lime. Lime and fluorine for Cancer sign; lime and phosphorous for Capricorn sign and lime and Sulphur for Scorpio.

Lime should never be used internally below 3rd decimal trituration.

The chemistry of Sagittarius:
November 22, 5 a.am., to December 21, 10 p.m.

The mineral or cell-salt of the blood corresponding to Sagittarius is silica.

Synonyms: silica, silici oxide, white pebble or common quartz. Chemical abbreviation SI. Made by fusing crude silica with carbonate of soda; dissolve the residue, filter, and precipitate by hydrochloric acid.

This product must be triturated as per biochemic process before using internally.

This salt is the surgeon of the human organism. Silica is found in the hair, skin, nails, periosteum, the membrane covering and protecting the bone, the nerve sheath, called neurilemma, and a trace is found in bone tissue. The surgical qualities of silica lie in the fact that its particles are sharp cornered. A piece of quartz is a sample of the finer particles. Reduce silica to an impalpable powder and the microscope reveals the fact that the molecules are still pointed and jagged like a large piece of quartz rock. In all cases, where it becomes necessary that decaying organic matter be discharged from any part of the body by the process of suppuration, these sharp pointed particles are pushed ceasing, day and night in the wonderous human Beth, and like a lancer cuts a passage to the surface for the discharge of pus. Nowhere in all the records of physiology or biological research can anything be found more wonderful than the chemical and mechanical operation of this divine artisan.

The bone covering is made strong and firm by silica. In case of boils or carbuncle, the biochemist loses no time searching for "anthrax bacilli" or germs, nor does he experiment with imaginary germ-killing serum, but simply furnishes nature with tools with which the necessary work may be accomplished.

The centaur of mythology is known in the "Circles of Beasts that worship before the Lord (Sun) day and night," as Sagittarius, the archer, with drawn bow. Arrow heads are composed of flint, decarbonized white pebble or quartz. Thus, we see why silica is the special birth salt of all born in the Sagittarius sign. Silica gives the glossy finish to hair and nails. A stalk of corn or straw of wheat, oats or barley would not stand upright except they contained this mineral.

Sagittarius people are generally swift and strong; and they are prophetic- look deeply into the future and hit the mark like the archer. A noted astrologer once said: "Never lay a wager with one born with the Sun in Sagittarius or *with Sagittarius rising in the East lest you lose your wealth."*

The Sagittarius native is very successful in thought transference. He (or she) can concentrate on a brain, miles distant, and so vibrant the aerial wires that fill space that the molecular intelligence of those finely attuned to nature's harmonies may read the message.

Governing planet, Jupiter.

Gems, carbuncle, diamond, turquoise.

The astral colors are gold, red and green.

Sagittarius is a fire sign and is represented in Bible alchemy by Levi, the third son of Jacob, meaning "joined or associated."

In the symbolism of the new testament, Sagittarius corresponds with the disciple James, son of Alpheus.

The Chicago Evening Post, Wednesday. August 19, 1914, in commenting on "Signs of Wrath and Portents from the heavens," says among other things: "And in England today are men with the Modern scientific mind who say that we cannot disregard utterly the idea that the movements of the heavenly bodies have their effects upon men.

Capricorn: *The Goat of the Zodiac:*
December 21, 10 p.m., to January 21, 3 a.m.

Circle means sacrifice, according to the cabal, the straight line bending to form a circle.

Thus, we find twelve zodiacal signs sacrificing to the sun. Symbolized by the devotions and sacrifices of the twelve disciples to Jesus.

Twelve months' sacrifice for a solar year.

Twelve functions of man's body sacrifice for the temple, Beth or "Church of God"-the human house of flesh.

Twelve minerals-known as cell-salts sacrifice by operation and combining to build tissue.

The dynamic force of these vitalized workmen constitute the chemical affinities-the positive and negative poles of mineral expression.

The cabalistic numerical value of the letters g, o, a, t, add up to 12.

Very ancient allegories depict a goat bearing the sins of Israelites into the wilderness.

In the secret mysteries of initiation into certain societies, the goat is the chief symbol.

In alchemical lore the "Great Work" is commenced. "In the Goat" and is finished in the "White Stone". Biochemistry is the "Stone the builders rejected" and furnishes the key to all mysteries and occultism of the allegorical goat.

Those persons born between the dates December 21 and January 21 come under the influence of the Sun in Capricorn-the Goat. Capricorn represents the great business interests-trusts and syndicates-where may laborers are employed. Thus, Capricorn symbolizes the foundation and frame-work of society-the commonwealth of human interests.

The bones of the human organism represent the foundation stones and framework of the soul's temple (soul of man's temple).

Bone tissue is composed principally of the phosphate of lime. Known as calcarean phosphate or calcium phosphate. Without proper amount of lime, no bone can be formed, and bone is the foundation of the body.

A building must first have a foundation before the structure can be reared. Thus, we see why the "Great Work" commences in the Goat. Lime is white-hence the "White Stone."

In the 2nd chapter and 17th verse of revelation may be found the alchemical formula of the "White Stone."

"To him that overcometh will I give to eat of the hidden manna, and will give him a White Stone, and in the Stone a new name written which no man knoweth saving he that receiveth it."

In the mountains of India. It is said, a tribe dwells, the priests of which claim that man's complete history from birth to death is recorded in his bones. These people say bones are secret archives, hence do not decay quickly as does flesh and blood.

When the molecules of lime phosphate fall below the standard, a disturbance often occurs in the bone tissue and the decay of bone known as caries of bone, commences. Phosphate of lime is the worker in albumen. It carries it to bone and uses it as cement in the making of bone.

So-called Bright's disease (first discovered in a man named Bright) is simply a putflow of albumen via kidneys, due to a deficiency of phosphate of lime.

When the goat salt is deficient in the gastric juice and bile ferments arise from undigested foods, acids from which find their way to synovial fluids in the joints of legs or arms or hands and often cause severe pains, but why the chemical operation, which is perfectly natural, should be called rheumatism passeth understanding.

Non-functional albumen, caused by a lack of lime phosphate, is the cause of eruptions, abscesses, consumption, catarrh and many so-called diseases.

But let us all remember that disease means not-at-ease, and that the words do not mean an entity of any kind, shape, size, weight or quality, but an effect caused by some deficiency of blood material, and that only.

Phosphate of lime should never be taken in crude form. It must be triturated to 6th X, according to the biochemic method, in milk sugar in order to be taken up by the mucous membrane absorbents, and thus carried into the circulation.

Capricorn people possess a deep interior nature in which they often dwell in the "Solitude of the Soul."

They scheme and plan and build air castles and really enjoy their ideal world. If they are sometimes talkative, their language seldom gives any hint of the wonderland of their imagination.

To that enchanted garden the sign, "No Thoroughfare," forever blocks the way.

The Capricorn gems are white onyx and moon stone. The astral colors are garnet, brown, silver-gray and black. Capricorn is an Earth sign.

In bible alchemy, Capricorn represents Judah, the fourth son of Jacob, and means "The Praise of the Lord." In the symbolism of the New Testament,

Capricorn corresponds with the disciple John.

The sign of the son of Man:

Aquarius
January 21, 3 a.m., to February 19, 5 p.m.

O age of man: Aquarius, transmuter of all things base. "Son of Man in the Heavens, with sun-illuminated face."

Our journey was long and weary, with pain and sorrow and tears, but now at rest in thy kingdom, we welcome the coming years.

Those born between the dates January 21 and February 19 are doubly blest, and babies to be born during that period for many years to come will be favored of the gods.

The solar system has entered the "Sign of the Sun of Man," Aquarius, where it will remain for over 2000 years. According to planetary revolutions the Sun passes through Aquarius once every solar year; thus we have the double influence of the Aquarius vibration from January 21 and February 19.

Air contains 78% of nitrogen gas, believed by scientists to be mineral in ultimate potency. Minerals are formed by the precipitation of nitrogen gas. Differentiation is attained by the proportion of oxygen and aqueous vapor (Hydrogen) that unites with nitrogen.

A combination of sodium and chlorine form the mineral known as common salt. This mineral absorbs water. The circulation or distribution of water in the human organism is due to the chemical action of the molecules of sodium chloride.

Crude soda cannot he taken up by mucous membrane absorbents and carried into the circulation. The sodium molecules found in the blood have been received from vegetable tissue which drew these salts from the soil in high potency.

The mineral or cell-salts, can also be prepared (and are prepared) in biochemic or homeopathic potency as fine as the trituration of nature's laboratory in the physiology of plant growth and then they are thoroughly mixed with sugar of milk and pressed into tablets ready to be taken internally to supply deficiencies in the human organism. A lack of the proper amount of these basic mineral salts (twelve in number) is the cause of all so-called disease.

Common table salt does not enter the blood, being too coarse to enter the delicate tubes of mucous membrane absorbents, but this does distribute water along the intestinal tract.

Aquarius is known in astrological symbol as "The Water Bearer." Sodium chloride, known also as natrum muriaticum, is also a bearer of water, and chemically corresponds with the zodiacal angle of Aquarius.

The term angle, or angel, of the Sun may also be used, for the position of the Sun at birth largely controls the vibration of blood.

So, then, we have sodium chloride as the "birth salt" of Aquarius people.

The governing planets are Saturn and Uranus; the gems are sapphire, opal and turquoise; the astral colors are blue, pink and nile green. Aquarius is an air sign.

In bible alchemy, Aquarius represents Dan. The fifth son of Jacob, and means "judgment," or "he that judges." In the symbolism of the New Testament, Aquarius corresponds with the disciple James.

Uranus, the revolutionary planet, known as the "Son of Heaven."

Pisces: *the fish that swim in the pure sea:*
February 19, 5 p.m., to March 20, 5 p.m.

Most everybody knows that Pisces means fishes, but few there be who know the esoteric meaning of fish. Fish in Greek is Ichthus, which Greek scholars claim means "substance from the sea."

Jesus is derived from the Greek for fish; Mary, Mare, means water; therefore, we see how the Virgin Mary, pure sea, gives birth to Jesus, or fish. There are two things in the universe—Jesus and the Virgin Mary—spirit and substance. So much for the symbol or allegory.

From the earth viewpoint we say that the Sun enters the Zodiacal sign

Pisces February 19 and remains until March 20. This position of the Sun at birth gives the native a kind, loving nature, industrious methodical, logical and mathematical; sympathetic and kind to people in distress.

In the alchemy of the bible we find that the sixth son of Jacob, Napthtali, which means "wrestling of God", symbolizes Pisces, for the Pisces natives worry and fret because they cannot do more for their associates or those in trouble.

The phosphate of iron is one of the cell-salts of human blood and tissue. This mineral has an affinity for oxygen which is carried into the circulation and diffused throughout the organism by the chemical force of this inorganic salt. The feet are the foundation of the body. Iron is the foundation of blood. Most diseases of Pisces people commence with symptoms indicating a deficiency of iron molecules in the blood; hence it is inferred that those born between the dates February 19 and March 20 use more iron than do those born in other signs.

Iron is known as the magnetic mineral, due to the fact that it attracts oxygen. Pisces people possess great magnetic force in their hands and make the best magnetic healers.

Health depends upon a proper amount of iron phosphate molecules in the blood. When these oxygen carriers are deficient, the circulation is increased in order to conduct a sufficient amount of oxygen to the extremities-all parts of the body with the diminished quantity of iron on hand.

This increased motion of blood causes friction, the result of which is heat. Just why this heat is called fever is a conundrum; maybe because fever is from Latin fever, "to boil out," but there seems to be no relevancy between a lack of phosphate of iron and "boiling out."

The phosphate of iron (ferrum phosphate),in order to be made available as a remedy for the blood, must be triturated according to the biochemic method with method with milk sugar up to the third or sixth potency in order that the mucous membrane absorbents may take it up and carry it into the blood. Iron in the crude state, like the tincture, does not enter the circulation, but passes off with the feces and is often an injury to the intestinal mucous membrane.

The governing planet is Jupiter.

The gems are chrysolite, pink-shell and moon stone.

The astral colors are white pink, emerald-green and black.

Pisces is a water sign.

In bible alchemy, Pisces represents Naphtali, the sixth son of Jacob, and means "wrestling's of God." In the symbolism of the New Testament, Pisces corresponds with the disciple Philip.

The birth of Benjamin is given in that wonderful allegory, the 35th chapter of Genesis. Benjamin is therefore, the 13th child of Jacob. See article, "13, the operation of wisdom," God-Man; The word made flesh.

INDIVIDUAL SALTS

1.	Calc Flour	No. 1	Tissue elasticity, impaired circulation, varicose veins; piles
2.	Calc Phos	No. 2	Debility; repaired digestion; teething trouble; chilblains
3.	Calc Sulph	No. 3	Acne, adolescent pimples; skin slow to heal; sore lips. A blood constituent
4.	Ferr Phos	No. 4	Blood stream oxygenation; chills; fevers; inflammation; congestion coughs; colds
5.	Kali Mur	No. 5	Minor respiratory ailments; coughs; colds; children's feverish ailments
6.	Kali Phos	No. 6	Nerve soothing, exhaustion, indigestion, headache; stress due to worry or exhaustion
7.	Kali Sulph	No. 7	Skin condition; skin eruptions with scaling or sticky exudations; falling hair; diseased nails; catarrh
8.	Mag Phos	No. 8	Cramp; neuralgia; flatulence; spasmodic nerve pains. A soft tissue constituent
9.	Nat Mur	No. 9	Maintaining body water distribution; watery colds, flow of tears; loss of smell
10.	Nat Phos	No. 10	Over acidity of the blood; gastric disorders; heartburn; rheumatic tendency
11.	Nat Sulph	No. 11	Water infiltrations; liverish symptoms; influenza; bilious attacks
12.	Silica	No. 12	Impure blood & for boils, brittle nails & lack-lustre hair

Chapter 7: Law and Order
*Rules and Regulations:

Universal laws-deal with energies/vibrations. Main principle: whatever energy you put out must come back to you.

Natural laws-deal with the natural ways of all objects and beings which have manifested in the 3rd dimension.

Tort laws-a wrongdoing should be, must be, will be made right.

Laws of Maxim-general truth and principle also known as God's laws. These laws come direct from God Th Creator from birth to death, the living soul free spirit, rights given by God to all beings and cannot be taken away by anyone in un alien able.

Sovereign-flesh and blood human beings master of self operates under God's laws of conscience, no one else, only sovereigns have the ability to create laws and constitutions for itself and corporations that it creates.

Contract law-maritime admiralty ecclesiastical canon law; a set of "laws" which "sovereigns" worldwide adhere to only in commerce in which an offer is made, if you accept it, you will then enter into a contract which means you are giving them jurisdiction over you. Offer + acceptance=contract.

Treaties-laws made between two sovereigns that deal with a particular tract of land.

Corporation-a dead fictitious entity straw-man operates under the laws of the constitution developed by the sovereign. Does not have the ability to create laws, can only create codes, statues and ordinances.

Federal codes-codes which govern corporations within corporations including Ucc's; policy enforcers/ agents; private agencies of corporations they belong to legally equivalent to a private citizen.

Citizen-a "slave/ p.o.w" of the corporation to which it pledges does not have rights only has legal privileges (license) which are given to it by the corporation to which it pledges.

20 Maxims of Equity:

Equity sees that as done what ought be done.

Equity will not suffer a wrong to be without a remedy.

Equity delights inequality.

One who seeks equity must do equity.

Equity aids the vigilant, not those who slumber on their rights.

Equity imputes an intent to fulfill an obligation.

Equity acts in personam or persons.

Equity abhors a forfeiture.

Equity does not require an idle gesture.

He who comes into equity must come with clean hands.

Equity delights to do justice and not by halves.

Equity will take jurisdiction to avoid a multiplicity of suits.

Equity follows law.

Equity will not aid a volunteer.

Where equities are equal, the law will prevail.

Between equal equities the first in order of time shall prevail.

Equity will not complete an imperfect gift.

Equity will not allow a statute to be used as a cloak for fraud.

Equity will not allow a trust to fail for want of a trustee.

Equity regards the beneficiary as the true owner.

*10 Native American Commandments:

Trust the Earth and all that dwell thereon with respect.

Remain close to the great spirit, in all that you do.

Show great respect for your fellow beings.

Work together for the benefit of all man.

Give assistance and kindness wherever needed.

Do what you know to be right.

Look after the well being of mind and body.

Dedicate a share of your efforts to the greater good.

Be truthful and honest always especially with self.

Take full responsibility for your actions.

7 Noahide Laws:

Noahide Laws

These Seven Universal Laws pertain to:
- **Avodah Zarah:** Prohibition on idolatry.
- **Birchat HaShem:** Prohibition on blasphemy and cursing the Name of God.
- **Shefichat Damim:** Prohibition on murder.
- **Gezel:** Prohibition on robbery and theft.
- **Gilui Arayot:** Prohibition on immorality and forbidden sexual relations.
- **Ever Min HaChay:** Prohibition on removing and eating a limb from a live animal.
- **Dinim:** Requirement to establish a justice system and courts of law to enforce the other 6 laws.

CHAPTER 8: RECONSTRUCTION OF UNITY
*Yoga Paths:

Union by knowledge-perspective

Union by devotion-faith

Union by action-experience; courage

Union by sound-vibration

Union by bodily control-discipline

Union by mental control-equanimity

*7 habits for hearing the heart:

Be still: to tune in to the heart, it is necessary to slow down, sit down, and quiet down. You don't need to assume any particular posture, but it is necessary to be still enough to take full notice of being in the present moment instead of getting ready for the next moment or to worrying about a wasted past moment. 13th century Christian mystic mister Eckhart said, "there is nothing in all creation so like God as stillness." Stop moving, stop thinking, don't try any particular gimmick or technique, and just be still for a few moments. One way to do this is to take a deep breath and sigh.

Lighten up: someone once said that the average being thinks he isn't average. Don't take yourself to seriously. You are not nearly as powerful and in control as your brain thinks you are or have to be. Most of the problems, accomplishments, and worries you experience at any given moment are transitory. And of very little relevance in the overall scheme of your life. A heart can become heavy both spiritually and in terms of the physiological changes associated with a relentless brain's burdens. Remember the insight of British author G.K. Chesterton who wrote, "Angels fly because they take themselves light."

Shut up: stop talking, and that includes talking to yourself. This is a vey difficult step because the brain is constantly gabbing about its 4 f's of feeding (or getting more stuff), fighting (or protecting its territory), fleeing (or moving on to somewhere else), and fornicating (or deriving intense and immediate physical pleasure). Try ignoring your brain for a while and just let it talk to itself. Try letting your own :hidden observer," that part of you that is always alert even when the brain is at rest, keep an eye on things while you relax. Ding and saying less is generally good for your mental, spiritual and physical health. Follow Oscar Wilde's advice when he pointed out, "I do not talk to God so as not to bore him."

Resonate: cardio-contemplation is a form of receptive prayer. It is not asking for something from or talking to a higher power but listening to the power within your heart. For its profound awareness of your connection with Th Creator. Physician Larry Dorsey writes, "In its simplest form, prayer is an attitude of the heart-a matter of being, not doing. Prayer is the desire to connect with the absolute, however it may be conceived. When we experience the need to enact this connection, we are praying.

Feel: you share your info-energy and cellular memories with every system in the cosmos. Don't tune out the world around you to tune in to your heart. Instead, be deeply aware and feel with all your senses your connection with the trees, flowers, water, or any natural system around you.

Learn: cardio-contemplation is learning from and by your heart. When we say we have learned something "by heart", we usually mean we have learned it well and lastingly. As you be still, lighten up, shut up, resonate, listen for what your heart is telling you about living, loving, and working. Try to store your lessons as cellular memories for later recall at the stressful times in your life.

Connect: try to send your lessons and the balanced "L" energy achieved in a cardio-contemplative state to the world around you and be open to incoming "L" energy coming from other hearts. Cardio-contemplation is a profound way to become a more complete part and healer of the world.

*Money will buy:

- A bed but not sleep.
- Books but not brains.
- Food but not an appetite.
- Finery but not beauty.
- A house but not a home.
- Medicine but not health.
- Luxuries but not a culture.
- Amusements but not happiness.
- A crucifix but not a savior.
- A church but not heaven.

*13 Firsts:

Love self-first: first know and respect yourself, then you can know, love and respect others.

Nation first: first love your own people first, as you would love yourself, then you can genuinely love others.

Family first: first fulfill family responsibilities, and then you can take care of other responsibilities.

Internal first: first value what is in you, your unit (family) and community, then value what is outside of you, your family and community.

Ma'at first: first make your heart perfect, and then you can cultivate/elevate your mind and body.

Deeds first: first value deeds, then words. What you do determines your worth.

Hard work first: first give your best work, then relax and accept praise and reward.

Simplicity first: first value the basics, then more complex things.

Strong first: first honor the strong, the righteous, the dedicated, the very best, and then the weak.

Small first: first attend to the small, then the vast.

Self-correction first: first criticize and correct yourself, then others.

Wisdom first: first seek knowledge, and then spiritually guided scientific action.

*10 Virtues of the aspirant/student:

Control of thoughts

Control of actions

Devotion of purpose

Have faith in the ability of (your) teacher to teach the truth.

Have faith in (yourself) to assimilate the truth.

Have faith in (themselves) to wield the truth

Be free from resentment under the experience of persecution

Be free from resentment under the experience of wrong

Cultivate the ability to distinguish between right and wrong; and

Cultivate the ability to distinguish between the real and the unreal.

*Virtues for community:

Unity of spirit-one Creator, one aim, one destiny-the community feels an invisible sense of unity. Each member is like a cell in the body. The group needs the individual and the individual needs the group. The community is like the Kemetic "ka", the universal spirit. The all and everything.

Trust, honesty and balance-everyone is moved to trust all and everyone else, by principle. There is no sense of discrimination or elitism. This trust assumes that everyone is innately well-intended.

Openness-the feeling of safety-people are open to each other unreservedly. This means that individuals' problems quickly become the community's challenge. Being open to each other depends on trust.

Love and caring-nurturing and sustaining-what you have is for everybody to share. This sense of communication diminishes egotistical behavior. To have, while other community members do not, is an expression of the people making up a society of their own.

Respect for elders-the foundation-elders are the pillars and the collective memory of the community. They hold the wisdom that keeps the community together. The young initiates are taught by them. Elders prescribe the rituals for various occasions and monitor the dynamics of the community. Elders are the bridge between yesterday and today. Community and Elder, together, project for the future.

Respect for nature-the Neter-the spirit of the divine Creator-the essence of life-nature is the principal source out of which all wisdom is learned. It is the place where initiation occurs. It is the place from where medicine comes. It nourishes the entire community.

*17 principles of Success:

Definitiveness of Purpose-the starting point of all achievement: before you can accomplish anything of significance, you must first adopt a definite major purpose and specific plan to make it happen. Everyday, focus on your most important objectives to reach them rapidly and confidently.

The mastermind alliance-only through the cooperation of others will you find success: more than a team or partnership, a mastermind alliance is a group of two or more people who combine their experience, specialized knowledge and ideas to reach a shared objective exponentially faster and with greater results than acting alone.

Applied faith-action is the requirement of all faith: faith is an active state of mind. When a plan comes through to your conscious mind, accept with appreciation and gratitude and act upon it at once. Don't hesitate, argue, worry or challenge that it is right. Simply act in good faith.

Going the extra mile-to expect more, you must do more: this dynamic principle is more than a motivational mantra; it's based on the law of compensation. The more value you bring to your career and your unit, the more you are rewarded with pay, appreciation and love.

Pleasing personality-your greatest asset or liability: your personality is the combination of your mental, spiritual and physical traits and habits that make you unique. With every personal and business engagement, you should display sincerity and courtesy as well as a pleasing tone of voice and a welcoming smile.

Personal initiative-the power that starts all action: personal initiative is the underlying foundation of everyone who achieves significance. The minute you have the drive and passion to think and act on your own, there's no limit to what you can accomplish.

Positive mental attitude-success attracts more process: always keep your mind positively focused on what you want most. Think about success, you attract success. Before you can reap the results from the other 16 principles, you must accurately adopt this one.

Enthusiasm-turn thoughts into actions: make a daily habit of displaying your burning desires as it radiates outwards and affects everyone around you. Enthusiasm is the instrument by which adversities and temporary defeats are changed into action and accomplishment.

Self-discipline-the bottleneck through which your mind/personal power must flow: before you can control your needs, you must control your thoughts. Self-discipline calls for balancing the emotions of your heart with the reasoning of your mind.

Accurate thinking-your most beneficial power available: you have complete control over your thoughts. The accurate thinker separates facts into two classes: important and unimportant. Spend your time focusing on the most important and reap extraordinary results.

Controlled attention-great achievements are the results of the focused mind: controlled attention leads to mastery in any type of human endeavor. As you concentrate on your major purpose, you project a clear picture of that purpose upon the conscious mind. Next, the subconscious mind takes over until you take action.

Teamwork-cooperation always pays high dividends: teamwork is harmonious cooperation that is willing, voluntary and free. When teamwork is applied to any problem or opportunity, success is inevitable. Generosity, fair treatment, courtesy and a willingness to serve are qualities of teamwork.

Learning from adversity and defeat-each setback is a seed of opportunity: most so-called problems and temporary defeats may prove to be a blissing/gift in disguise. Because what grows from adversity are powerful life lessons that form the steps to success. Defeat is never "failure" until you believe it to be so.

Creative vision-unleash your imagination upon the world: you are far more creative, imaginative and inventive than you may give yourself credit for. Learn how to tap into your most creative abilities. The resulting ideas, solution and results will literally astound you.

Maintenance of sound health-your most valuable asset: you have nothing without your health. Your sound health begins in your mind-your health consciousness. Just as the right foods and exercise can prevent disease and increase your lifespan, so can the right healthy thoughts.

Budgeting time and finance-maximize these valuable, finite resources: where will you be in 5, 10, 20 years? You already know. Simply consider how you spend your spare time and how you spend your finance if your time and finance are spent on your unit, on improving yourself and by helping others, you will achieve greatness.

Cosmic habit force-fulfill your dreams….automatically: beyond mere habits, cosmic habit force engages universal laws where you automatically do what's right. Cultivating positive habits leads to peace of mind, health and financial security.

Chapter 9: Awakening
*Gaining:

If you want this	You need this
· strength	· flexibility
· resiliency	· patience
· success	· failure
· expansion	· grounding
· knowledge	· learning
· wisdom	· intuition

*3 steps to religious practice:

Myth: converting the science of the cosmological forces into things that can be comprehended by a young mind; the art of anthropomorphic and zoomorphic constructs designed to bring about Innerstanding, relativity and interest in divine teachings.

Mysticism: the actual science that the myth/math represents and how it correlates and corresponds to what we see, think and feel; bridges the gap between the corporal and incorporeal; self-realization.

Ritual: the actual application of the knowledge gained which allows the art of manifesting divine energies to occur; the science of mastery i.e. the learned manipulating of Th Cosmic energies that are essentially reflections of ourselves, and the divine spark of brilliance innately housed within each of us, the act of self-actualization.

*3 steps of attaining of wisdom:

Listening: involves or rather is one with an open heart and mind; unbiased or doesn't allow their bias to stunt their growth; awareness of the value of knowledge both external and internal, knowing the meanings and picking up on the hidden meanings.

Reflection: critical thinking; ability to be objective which is to step outside of ego so as to properly assess what is digested; putting any and all knowledge to the test i.e. your common sense so as to gauge the logic of it; being able to see your failures as well as your triumphs.

Meditation: stilling the mind so that it may rest and be restored; allowing your personal inventory of amalgamated knowledge to be washed clean by superior divine intellect and wisdom; the gaining of supreme insight, which is ultimately, if accepted and properly manifested, Peace.

*3 needs of human beings:

Food: sustenance meaning both on the obvious sense of nutrition but also implies higher learning. As food nourishes the body so does higher spiritual learning nourish and nurture the spirit of man which leads to the blossom of soul.

Shelter: implies physical domicile i.e. house, hut, apartment etc., but also implies a community of like-minded and like spirited individuals who help elevate each other by way of sharing and caring.

Opportunity: everybody has a talent thus everyone has an innate need to express and expand that talent for the betterment of themselves and the people within their sphere of association and influence. So long as all skills are nurtured the structure of society cannot crumble for every man is a cornerstone, a master of their abilities and confident and content within themselves by virtue of being in alignment with their divine attributes and purpose.

*6 chambers (attributes) of the heart:

Fearlessness: fear robs man of the indomitability of his soul, disrupting nature's harmonious workings emanating from the source of divine power within. It causes physical, mental, and spiritual disturbances; continued anxieties give rise to psychological complexes and chronic nervousness. It ties the mind and heart (feeling) to the external (body) man, causing their consciousness to be stagnated, thus keeping man centered on ego, the body and anything that could potentially threaten the feigned security of them. The best advice is caution along with courage-fearlessness in spirit without rashly exposing oneself to unnecessary risks or to conditions that may arouse appearances. Everyone is given ample opportunities, without willfully creating them, to demonstrate courage and prove the power of faith. Death is perhaps the ultimate change of faith in mortal men. Fear of the inevitable is supremely foolish. It comes only once in a lifetime; and after it has come the experience is over, without having affected our true identity in any way or diminishing in any way our real being; however, it does shine a light on the deeds done; no one escapes karma.

Purity: means sincerity and transparency to truth. One's consciousness of attachment and repulsion to sense objects. Likes and dislikes for externals taint the heart with gross vibrations resulting in egotism, lust, greed and emptiness.

Steadfastness: seeking with the utmost sincerity divine wisdom and practicing and embodying the higher spiritual qualities of divine self; is essential for liberation. In their daily life, the aspirant/devotee should apply the ancient ancestral wisdom gained by scripture, Innerstanding and external instructions from those are pure and certified to give divine intervention and guidance. Doing so immerses one in the peace born of application. Wisdom guards the devotee, by right reason and perception from falling into pits of ignorance and sense pleasures,

He Charity: is meritorious and expands the consciousness. Unselfishness and generosity link the soul of the open-handed giver to the presence of God within all other souls. It destroys the delusion of personal ownership in this dream drama of life, whose sole possessor is the cosmic dreamer. The bounty of Th Earth is merely on loan to us from Th Creator. That which Th Most High has given into our keeping is judiciously used when it serves the needs and removes the suffering of one's self and others. The true devotee spontaneously, from hi expanded heart, desires to share with others his possessions, knowledge, and soul insight.

Self-restrain and discipline: power to control the senses when they are excited by the pleasant sensations of sight, hearing, smell, taste, or touch. A devotee who is master of his senses is ready for emancipation. He who succumbs to temptations will remain entangled in sense objects, far removed from soul knowledge. Every indulgence in any form of sense-lures reinforces the desire for that experience. Repetition leads to the formation of nearly unshakeable bad habits.

Rituals and religious rites: a devotee, no matter what level or state of development, must perform the mental rite of burning wrong desires in the flames of wisdom, and consuming restlessness in the fire of soul ecstasy. The whole of one's life should be a Yajna (sacrifice by fire), with every thought and act purified by a devout heart and offered as oblation to Th Most High Supreme Creator.

*7 stages of awakening:

Creator: aspirations; intent of will; seeing clearly your purpose

Scribe: gain intellect through study; codifying inner wisdom; assimilation of external and internal knowledge and perception

House of light: logical step of progressive study and self-reflection; confidence gained and earned; flow and conduit of energy

Eternal soul: self-realization; activation of the 1st eye; enhanced perception and metaphysical abilities

Wisdom: intuition gained by experience; refinement

Light: aura field is up; earning your wings; golden glow; transcendent; ophidian (serpent) pharos (beacon)

Sage: qualified and certified master; bestower of knowledge and wisdom; healer; redeemer; leader; true servant of Th Universe; royal/sovereign

*8 Qualities of a Sage:

- Liberality
- Acceptance
- Patience
- Capacity to communicate by symbols
- Estrangement from their own people
- Modest garb
- Traveler
- Humility

*Postulates of the Sages:

All things are thought: all life is thought-activity. The multitudes of beings are but phases of the One great thought made manifest. Lo, Allah is thought, and thought is Allah.

Eternal thought is one: in essence it is two-fold - intelligence and force; and, when they breath a child is born; this child is love. And thus, the triune Allah stands forth, whom men call father, mother and son. This triune Allah is One;but like the One of light, in essence is seven. And when the triune Allah breathes forth, Lo, seven spirits stand before his face. These are creative attributes. Men call them lesser Gods and in their image made man.

Man Mortal: was a thought of Allah formed in the image of the septonate, clothed in the substance of soul. And his desires were strong. He sought to manifest on every plane of life. And for himself he made a body of the ethers of the earthly forms; and so, he descended to the plane of earth. In this descent he lost his birthright, lost his harmony with Allah, made discordant all the notes of life. Inharmonious and evil are the same. So evil is the handiwork of man.

Timing and precision: seeds do not germinate in light. They do not grow until they find the soil and hide themselves away from light. Man was/is an evolved seed of everlasting life; but in the ethers of the triune Allah, the light was far too great for seeds to grow. And so man sought the soil of carnal life; and in the darkness of earth he found a place where he could germinate and grow. The seed has taken root and grown full well. The tree of life is rising from the soil of earthly things, and, under natural law, is reaching up to perfect form. There is no supernatural acts of Allah to lift man from carnal life to spirit blissfulness. He grows as grows the plant; and, in due time is perfected. The quality of soul that makes it possible for man to rise to spirit life is purity.

Chapter 10: Rulership
*7 Laws of Teaching:

(1) Law of preparation:

(A) The teacher must know the content of the lesson to be taught.

(B) The teacher must prepare to communicate the content and message of the lesson.

(C) Methodical Lesson Preparation:

    Personal study of the lesson content.

    Thorough planning of the teaching process.

    Careful selection of teaching materials.

    Adept selection of teaching methods.

    Thorough development.

(D) The teacher should utilize proper tools for his/her preparation (bibles, dictionary, commentaries, atlas, etc.). This is where the teacher's library can be helpful.

(E) 5 practical questions the teacher should ask himself/herself:

    What do I want my pupils to know?

    What do I want my pupils to feel?

    What do I want my pupils to do?

    What choices do I want my pupils to make?

    What kind of character should my pupils manifest?

(F) Prepare your materials:

Pictures	Projected aids
Objects	Clippings
Flannel graph	Etc

(G) Prepare your methods:

Lecture	Discussion
Storytelling	Question and answer
Recitation	

(2) The law of pupil:

(A) formally stated, the law is: the pupil must attend with interest to the material being taught.

(B) 3 types of attention:

　The attention may be voluntary.

　The attention may be coerced.

　The attention may be absorbing (oblivious to his/her surroundings).

(3) Law of the language:

(A) The language used in teaching must be common to both teacher and pupil.

(B) The same meaning must be evident to both before good communication is possible.

(C) The vocabulary of the teacher must be adapted to that of the pupil. Otherwise, the use of words foreign to the pupil's understanding will prohibit the pupil from receiving the message of the lesson.

(4) the law of the lesson:

(A) Truth to be taught must be learned through truth already known

(B) Yashuah utilized this approach:

　Parables

　He compared physical water with spiritual water.

　He compared doors with himself as the way to heaven.

　Remember the K.I.S.S (keep it simply said) principle.

(5) The law of the teaching process:

(A) The teacher must motivate and guide the student.

(B) The teacher must help the student be a discoverer of truth. Although you already know where it is hidden, lead the student to discover the golden egg.

(C) The teaching process demands student participation.

(6) The law of the learning process:

(A) There are at least 5 steps in the learning process:

    Memorization

    Understanding/Innerstanding/overstanding

    Expressing the thought

    Giving evidence of beliefs

    Application of knowledge in daily life.

(B) It is useful for the student to bear 5 questions in mind during the period of study:

    What does the lesson mean?

    How can I express the lesson in my own words?

    How can I use this knowledge?

(7) The law of review and application:

(A) This law is based on the demands of the mind for frequent reviews of the lessons learned.

(B) Frequent reviews are practical for both student and teacher.

Neophyte training: 1st degree

*Working Tool of the 1st level:

24-inch gauge: is taught that by the 24 inch gauge he should divide his time: 8 hours for the service of God and a distressed worthy being. 8hours for your vocation (work) and 8 hours for rest and refreshment.

The common gavel: an "ashlar" is a stone. The common gavel was used by entered apprentice operative Masons to break the corners off of a rough stone (rough ashlar) to better craft them to the builder's purpose....to lay a true and correct foundation of a building.

Without "perfect ashlars" with which to lay your personal foundation, your building cannot be laid out on the square, nor be perfectly plumbed, upright.

What do all freemen seek? Light. "Light" represents knowledge. All freemen continually seek knowledge. Symbolizes beginnings and orientations.

Fellowcraft training: 2nd degree:

Symbolism: methods of developing the mind and progressing in craft, in a larger sense, the emergence into symbolic manhood, maturity, and its commensurate responsibilities.

*Working tools:

The plumb: an instrument made use of by operative stone masons to try perpendiculars and to see that the rising courses of the stone are true to the cornerstone and to the center of the earth. Speculatively it symbolizes moral rectitude, of uprightness of conduct, of living an ethical and "good" life, and acting on the straight and narrow path of truth, justice, and mercy; placing fairness and honest dealing above personal gain and profit.

The square: an instrument made use of by operative stone masons to "square" their work to what is true with respect to the foundation and the cornerstone of the building. To the speculative mason, the square symbolizes morality, truthfulness, and honesty. The direction of the two sides of the square form an angle of 90 degree, or a right angle, so-called because this is the angle which stones must have if they are to be used to build a stable and upright wall. It symbolizes accuracy, not varying by even a single degree. We may travel in different directions (physically), but with full knowledge that our various courses in life will be guided according to the angle of the square (which means the right direction), until we meet again.

The level: an instrument made use of by operative stonemasons to prove and determine horizontals. To the speculative mason, it symbolizes equality. Each being is endowed with worth and dignity which is truly spiritual and should not be subject to man-made distinctions. Some men may have greater potential in life, service, or reward than other; but we know that any man can aspire to any height, no matter how great. Thus, the level dignifies physical as well as mental labor and the man who performs it. Also symbolizes the passage of time, which, in the final analysis, will level us all when we are at least called from earthly labor to face the supreme being and have our life's work reviewed; in Th Most High's eyes, we are equal.

The Pillars and The Porch: two pillars represent strength and establishment — and by implication, power and control. One must remember that power and control are placed before you, so that you might come to realize that power without control is anarchy, or conversely, that control without power and control if his life is to be successful. The two pillars also correspond to the three great supports of masonry-wisdom, strength and beauty. The pillars of wisdom and strength are represented by the pillars in the North and South, respectively, and the initiate, as he matures and grows in spiritual attunement, comes to symbolize the 3rd column - that of beauty, or balance — three legs being infinitely more stable than two.

*Wages of 2nd level: corn, wine and oil.

Corn-nourishment and the sustenance of life. A symbol of plenty and refers to the opportunity for doing good, working for the community, and performing service to man and mankind.

Wine-refreshment, health and peace.

Oil-spirituality, joy, gladness and happiness.

The actual "wages" of the modern-day masons are the intangible, but no less real, compensation for faithful and intelligent use of one's working tools, fidelity to one's obligations, and unflagging interest in the study of the structure, purpose, possibility of unity.

*3 precious jewels:
   The attentive ear   The instructive tongue   The faithful breast

*4 cornerstones of study and contemplation:
   Numbers — 7 liberal arts; divination   Symmetry — balance
   Order — intellect; discipline   Proportion — justice; honor

*3 forms of knowledge:
Intellectual: information and the collection of facts, and the use of these to arrive at further intellectual concepts. This is intellectualism.

States: includes both emotional feeling and strange states of being in which man thinks that he has perceived something supreme but cannot avail self of it. This is emotionalism.

Real knowledge: called knowledge of reality. In this form, man can perceive what is right, what is true, beyond the boundaries of thought and sense.

Scientists and scholastics concentrate upon the first form of knowledge.

Emotionalists and experimentalists use the second form.

Others use two combined, or either alternatively.

But the people who attain to truth are those who know how to connect themselves with the reality which lies beyond both these forms of knowledge.

*Methods of effective teaching: Expanding Consciousness
   Auditory, visual and other sense-impacts.

Verbalized materials, including legends and parables, intended to establish in the mind not a belief but a pattern, a blueprint which helps it to operate in 'another' manner.

Working, worshiping, exercising, in unison, for the purpose of engineering, liberating and making flow a certain dynamic (not an emotional or indoctrination one) which furthers the 'work'.

The employment of places, objects, symbols and so on, which are held to supplement ordinary human cognitions, not to train them.

The organizing of local and other groups, composed of people chosen because of the inherent possibility of their harmonizing in an esoteric community, to encourage the development of something within the community; not a community magnetized around an idea.

The selection, from traditional or other formulations, of practices and procedures solely by the criterion of function. Will this work successfully, given a certain type of being in a certain culture?

The creation of working communities by selecting locally approved vocational and other groupings which can be also of use in the dervish 'work'. The introduction of grouping-systems which may be lacking in the local culture, because they have no psychological appeal or no economic validity.

The production of procedures, techniques and materials which may be used to make contact with the inner aspect of a being, without disrupting his habitual activities without disrupting his habitual activities based upon local or temporal conditioning. Mystic operation is therefore a highly skilled and complex endeavor. The major characteristics of well-known Sufi (mystic) school-dancing, jumping, listening to and playing music and the like are all popularizations ignorantly initiated from an originally very sophisticated 'technology' whose expertise is the instant knowledge of the teachers as to which process applies to what circumstances.

*Standings:

Overstanding — where man's perception must reach into the heights for comprehension.

Understanding — where the perception of man reach into the depths for comprehending.

Innerstanding — where the perception of man must reach into the width of situations for comprehension.

Outstanding — where the perception of man must reach at length into situations for comprehension.

*Fate and action:

If you have not heeded and applied what has been offered to you, much confusion and unnecessary suffering will follow you. Your own actions will cause these events, until you learn.

You will have to travel:

From profligatory (wastefulness) to ill-luck;

From despair to insufficient remedy;

From carelessness to derision;

From misery to desperation;

From obedience to fulfillment;

From testing to enlightenment.

*Sufi and scholars:

These scholars may often be regarded as decorative and useful people. Their decorative and utilitarian aspects, however, should be clearly perceived, in accordance with the principle that misunderstandings and distortions always occur when something is not defined which could be defined.

They frequently desire attention and do all they can to get it. They do not seek to propagate their ideas so much as to require that people think that they are being scholars.

Like containers, and permutation, accumulation and analysis agents of various kinds, they are able for the most part, to hold, to preserve, even to pass on-but not effect any real change in-the materials with which they are concerned. A limited scholar who translates a book, for instance, may be giving its contents to someone who can absorb it, like a jug which contains water which will ultimately by others.

Scholars of a lesser sort, however, being human and not animal or inanimate, sometimes tend to confuse their own desires with their real effect and possible functions. This is only because they may have an image of themselves which has been fostered without being investigated.

Scholars cannot readily be studied by other scholars, who are by virtue of their involvement unlikely to be able to attain sufficient objectivity.

Scholars, however, can be studied by Sufis. There are innumerable Sufis who have once been scholars: but there is no single Sufi, perhaps in all history, who has subsequently become a scholar. Scholarship, therefore, may be regarded as which it is not. If, for instance, one were to believe that bread and milk were the only true and valuable forms of food, it could mean that those who ate bread and milk might imagine that they had perceived and were operating at the apogee of nutrition. On the other hand, where there are other nutritions available, and when these are superior in some or many respects to those which are only supposed to be the solitary or best ones, a critical situation exists.

*4 modes of escape (ism):
- North-intellectual (ism)
- South-sexual (ism)
- East-spiritual (ism)
- West-social (ism)

*5 requirements for the attaining of balance through service:
The being must be able to allow that the foregoing analysis may be correct.

One must familiarize self with the argument, remembering that shallower contentions about analysis of situations and the nature of service are already rooted in his brain.

They must realize that merely supposing that one innerstands/overstands the foregoing is often simply a prelude to forgetting it.

One has to undergo specialized exercises which help to make it possible for the brain to work consistently in another manner as well as in the conventional one which is now customary to it.

One must examine self to see whether they are expecting too much from their studies or from life in the immediate reward sense, and hence being forced to devour valuable experiential nutrition as emotional stimulus to assuage the tensions caused by his random expectations.

*Sufi Wisdom:
Tell the truth, even if on your own selves.

If you were to stay sober it would be better for you.

To be without one's senses is no repose. He cannot be called wise who leads men to senselessness.

Rather, one should seek out that which increases reason and wisdom.

Those who go out in search of knowledge will be in the path of God until they return.

Laughter will take you to the gates of heaven but not through them.

Courtesy is neither to quarrel nor to submit blindly, but to share. Courtesy is reciprocity, harmony, the art of living with others to the mutual benefit of self and others.

Outro:

Much respect and appreciation to you the reader for your attention. It is my sincere hope that you have gained something valuable from this assortment of philosophy that will propel you forward on your quest or at the very least give you a sense of equilibrium that will empower you towards your righteous destiny. Peace, prosperity, power and protection on you and your noble house.

Works Cited:

Idries Shah. 2017. *Learning How to Learn : Psychology and Spirituality in the Sufi Way.* London: Isp Publishing.

Shah, Idries. 2019. *Way of the Sufi.*

"Spirituality before Religions with Kaba Hiawatha Kamene." n.d. Www.youtube.com. Accessed April 24, 2022. https://www.youtube.com/watch?v=CQCIfwvTacg.

Pearsall, Paul. 1999. The Heart's Code : Tapping the Wisdom and Power of Our Heart Energy. New York: Broadway Books.

Lansdowne, Zachary F. 1993. The Chakras & Esoteric Healing. Delhi: Motilal Banarsidass.

Muata Abhaya Ashby, and Asha. 1994. TemT Tchaas : Ancient Egyptian Proverbs, Teachings and Meditations. Miami, Fla.: Cruzian Mystic Books.

Afrika, Llaila O. 2000. Nutricide : The Nutritional Destruction of the Black Race. Buffalo, New York: Eworld Inc.

Afrika, Llaila O. 2004. African Holistic Health. Buffalo, N.Y.: Eworld, Inc.

Royal, Penny C. 1982. Herbally Yours. Payson, Utah: Sound Nutrition.

"The Zodiac & Salts of Salvation." n.d. Www.rvbeypublications.com. Accessed Feb 24, 2022. http://www.rvbeypublications.com/catalog/i40.html.

Fillmore, Charles. 1995. The Twelve Powers of Man. Unity Village, Mo.: Unity Books, Printing.

"The Oracle." n.d. Www.rvbeypublications.com. Accessed Feb 24, 2022. http://www.rvbeypublications.com/catalog/i44.html.

Support Your Own!!!

- Califamedia.com (literature and publishing)
- Rvbeypublications.com (literature)
- DrAlimElBey.com (herbs, crystals, literature and More)
- Moorsandmasonry.org (etymology, history, jurisprudence and more)
- Moreignaheir.com (Moorish American Apparel)
- WillofAllah.com (music)
- Riseofthemoors.org
- 13krystalign.com (Detoxes and Cleanses)
- Uprisingtea.com
- Obashangoel.com
- Ledhealthy.com
- Moorsinfulllife.com
- Knovaarts.com
- Tune-earth.com
- Knovaarts.com
- Kemajikgems.com
- Fezdealer.com

www.ingramcontent.com/pod-product-compliance
Lightning Source LLC
Chambersburg PA
CBHW030154100526
44592CB00009B/271